Penguin Education

Story The second book
an anthology of stories and pictures
edited by David Jackson and Dennis Pepper

Story
the second book

an anthology of stories and pictures
edited by
David Jackson and Dennis Pepper

Penguin Books

Penguin Books Ltd, Harmondsworth,
Middlesex, England
Penguin Books Inc, 7110 Ambassador Road,
Baltimore, Md 21207, USA
Penguin Books Australia Ltd,
Ringwood, Victoria, Australia

First published 1973
This selection copyright © David Jackson and Dennis Pepper, 1973

Made and printed in Great Britain by
Butler and Tanner Ltd, Frome and London
Set in Lumitype Baskerville

Contents

Remember

Extracts from an autobiography

Locking Grandma in a cupboard

My earliest memory was when I locked my grandma in the cupboard. When I was a little girl and my mother was expecting my brother, my grandma came to our house for the day. Under the stairs we had a cupboard in which we kept our brushes and mops. My grandma had gone into the cupboard for something, and as I had a habit of closing doors I saw the door open and just shut it, I then ran out to play. When my grandma found out she was locked in she started to shout. Hearing her upstairs my mother said she would get up and let her out. My grandma not allowing my mother to get up said she would wait there till my dad came home.

My mum sat thinking what she could do when she heard the old man next door, she shouted out of the window for him. She told him to let my grandma out of the cupboard, so he let her out. When he came in I got a clout but everybody thought it was funny.

A wooden puppet

The next thing I remember in my younger days is a wooden puppet that the next-door neighbour made. Mrs Tattersall called me into their house and said she had something for me. Gladly I ran into

her house thinking she'd been baking again (as she always gave me
something when she'd baked). I ran into the kitchen and it was a
wooden puppet which was sitting on an old worn table in the
middle of the room. I took the puppet off the table and ran home
to show my mum.

I was very pleased with the puppet. I took it everywhere with me,
until one day I had a fight with my eldest sister and she threw the
puppet on the fire. I can remember crying for ages until my mum
said I could have another. That shut me up so I went and boasted to
my sister that I was getting another, she said she'd burn that too if
she got hold of it but I never got another puppet so how could she
burn it?

Standing in the chimney

I can remember when my auntie Elsie and my uncle Billy were leaving Whitworth to go and live at Littlehampton. I was very fond of
my auntie and Billy so I didn't want them to leave. Before they went
my mum asked my auntie and Billy in for a cup of tea and a chat.
Everybody was sitting in the back having a drink when I disappeared. It was time for them to leave. When my auntie asked
where I was, nobody knew. My auntie said she wouldn't go without
saying goodbye to me. Everybody started to look for me.

7

I was standing in the front room with my head up the chimney. I can remember the soot clogging up my throat. It was my mum who found me. She told me later she could see two little black legs in the fireplace. She got me out of the chimney with some difficulty. My face was black and streaked with pink where I'd been crying. I told my mum I didn't want then to leave. My auntie came in and told me not to cry. I would go down to see her every year. I said goodbye and off she went in the little black car with Billy. After that we went to my auntie's every year for nine years.

A broken pot doll

One Christmas I woke up to find a large pot doll in a pram at the bottom of my bed, I took the doll everywhere with me. One morning I got up and took the doll out of its cot and laid it in my bed. Carefully I covered the doll up and went down stairs. All of a sudden I heard a crash from upstairs. I ran upstairs thinking that Christine (my sister) had knocked over a vase. There on the bedroom floor lay my doll in at least two dozen pieces. I can't say the feelings that went through my body. All I knew was that my doll was dead. I picked up the pieces and took them into the garden and buried them. I came into the house and managed not to cry.

It happened that Christine was bouncing on the bed and the doll had fallen off. I never forgave Christine for that.

I kept its clothes in a little box, and I only let my best dolls wear them. One day I found them on one of our Christine's dolls. I was that mad that I ripped them up and burned them.

LYNNE WHITEHEAD *aged 13*

Accident

I gleaned all my boyhood. I ran away from it once but came to grief, and since the results have been with me all my life, I will tell you about it. When I was six I got fed up with being in the gleaning-field with all the women, so I ran off to help the boy who worked the cattle-cake machine. In no time my hand was caught and my fingers were squashed. The farmer was just coming up by the granary on his horse when he heard me screaming. 'What have you been up to, you young scamp?' he shouted. 'My fingers – they're in the cake-breaker!' And he said – I shall never forget it – 'Get you off home then!' But when he saw my hand he changed his tune and said, 'Get up to the house.' The farmer's wife tied some rag round my hand and took me home and my mother wheeled me miles to the doctor's in a pram. My sister was home from service, so she came with us and held me while the doctor scraped the grease out of my wounds with a knife, stitched up one finger, cut another, pared it like a stick and tied what was left to the bone, and then moved on to the next finger. I lifted the roof, I can tell you. There was no anaesthetic, nothing. My sister began to faint and the doctor got on to her something terrific. 'Damn silly girl – clear off outside if you can't stand it! Fetch my groom in.' So the groom came and held me until it was finished. All the time the doctor worked he shouted. 'What did you do it for? Why? Damn little nuisance! Stupid little fool!'

Nobody used pity then, and especially not to children, and particularly not to boys. The farmer told my father and he said, 'I'll give him something to think about when I get home!' It was harvest so it was late when he returned. 'Where's that boy Leonard?' he said, 'I'm going to give him a good hiding.' 'He's gone to bed, he's had enough,' said mother. My father didn't realize how bad it was, you see. The tops of three of my fingers had been cut off. So he didn't touch me.

LEONARD THOMPSON

Christmas Party

'Oh George, look, Father Christmas isn't really Father
Christmas but Mr Thornley.' How sad we felt when we
saw him standing at the schoolroom door shouting at
the top of his voice, 'Fetch my cane, Willie
Murgatroyd, and get off the table, Sam Wilkins.' It
was a dreadful school party. Two of the teachers were
ill, so Aunt Frances asked Mother to help and bring us

along (also Gyp and Barney). But we couldn't stop
Willie Murgatroyd and Sam Wilkins from fighting, and
Annie urged them on. One little girl came to Mother
and said, 'Please, Miss, our Billy's wet his pants
and I feel sick.' 'Frances,' called Mother, 'what do we
do with her, she may be beginning with something . . .'

HELEN BRADLEY

In the Factory

I was fifteen. I remember being intimidated at first by the sprawling, prison-like buildings, the intent look of people going in and the grim faces of the works' police. I was taken into the concrete box with slits for windows and told to sit down and wait. Two men were inside, and as there was hardly any space, the sourness was very strong. One of the men glanced up from pouring tea into a chipped cup. I was sitting right against him. My gaze strayed around and I saw the long row of keys over his head, all labelled and hung on brass hooks. The other man had squatted down, jamming his knees under the little table where there was a phone, and my brand-new insurance card was sticking up unnaturally in his beefy hand. He was squinting at it with great concentration, waiting, and then somebody must have answered. He shouted angrily into the mouthpiece that he had a new apprentice with him, pronouncing my surname wrongly. He listened again, scowling, then suddenly slammed the phone down as if disgusted.

I followed him out, feeling ridiculous and pathetic because of the neat bundle I was clutching, which had my new overall and my sandwiches in it. Nothing was worse than being a beginner. We passed between the dismal low sheds stretching ahead endlessly, past holes in the walls, and doorways, entering and leaving the different smells. I caught a glimpse of a square orange fire, deep inside one of the places, and saw some dark burrowing figures. Then a man in a filthy boiler-suit came into the road ahead of us, pushing a barrowful of steel cuttings. The steel ribbons were brown and in rapid spirals, short and long pieces, tangled like snakes. He pushed them across, a high swaying heap, and disappeared.

We went along the side of a pool of stagnant water, about twenty paces square, edged with tubular railings, the surface coloured and veined with oil. Going past, my guide spoke for the first time since we had set out.

'Over this way,' he said, because he had turned sharply and I was not quick enough. Then after a few yards: 'In here.' He lumbered down a short, narrowing passage which ended in a blue door.

Until this moment he had been almost swaggering along, big-chested, aggressive, but now he seemed to shrink and become timid. He leaned on the door carefully, opening it with his shoulder. I was filled with foreboding at the sight of his sudden respect. Then he led me into the training centre and I was astonished because it looked so small and orderly, in the flood of bright light.

In the supervisor's office, after I closed the door on the noise, there was a curious numbed silence. I heard a faint drone, as if from something a long way off, and that was all. Through the glass sides I saw lads opening and shutting their mouths, bending over silent machines, banging away noiselessly with hammers. I noticed them while I waited for the supervisor to speak. He looked up from his papers reluctantly and said a few words, moving his bottom jaw sideways like a cow chewing. He had a thick Scottish accent. I started to reply, and with his eyes fixed on my face he lifted one arm and waved it about. This was a signal for one of the charge-hands to come in and attend to me.

I understood things, but it was like living in a cloud. After a few hours the surroundings were sharper, though it took days for them to be real.

We were in a corner of one of the main sheds, in a kind of special pen, half wooden and half wire mesh. You stood by the mesh and looked through at men and women, many of them smoking. The machines out there were massive, dwarfing ours. Every so often they gave hideous shrieks and groans. But there was only bluish fog hanging over them, and occasional handfuls of white sparks jumping out from the bottoms of grinding-wheels. Things were dirtier, more casual and realistic, that was the difference. The lofty roof and the space made it seem more heartless. I was glad to be where I was, but the squalor on that side of the fence was more alive and it attracted me.

If a girl saw us squinting through she would wave, and one of the men would notice and shout across to his mate, showing his teeth in a laugh. The white barriers which penned us in were a joke.

Our two charge-hands had been told not to swear in front of us. When the tea came, they sat squashed in their cubby-hole of an office, whispering and glancing out furtively. Their names were Morgan and Stokes. The youngest apprentices said 'sir' to them, as if speaking to schoolteachers.

Mr Morgan fascinated me. He was a tall, fair-headed Welshman with a lumpy, bulging forehead. He took strict, fastidious steps. Nobody trusted him, he was accepted as a deceitful person, yet he was popular. He stuck down his hair with grease and kept a pencil behind his ear. His overall pockets were full of junk. From behind he looked slovenly, his frayed trousers dropping over his heels.

If you happened to be talking and he spotted you he would sidle up and press between you cunningly, making it seem accidental; or he would say: 'All right, lads? No trouble?' Looking into his face you would find it blandly innocent, but with the eyes smirking.

I did not like Mr Stokes at all. He had a fat neck, a black thinned-down moustache, and his black hair was cropped short like a wrestler's. He was crude and shambling. He stood with his legs apart and looked across with little cynical eyes, rocking on his heels.

Once I was working on a bench lathe near a boy who had been brought in one Monday morning three weeks earlier, staring hard without comprehension as I must have done, shepherded by the same policeman. Now Mr Stokes stood behind him idly, watching, when suddenly the drill snapped. I heard the small crunching sound myself. Mr Stokes stepped forward and said: 'That another sod gone?'

'Yes,' the boy stammered. His hand that had been guiding the drill forward was fluttering about aimlessly.

'You dozy bastard,' Mr Stokes said.

The boy lost control and broke down. Crying hopelessly, he dragged at a white handkerchief, struggling to pull it out of his trouser pocket while he turned his head away, utterly disgraced. Apprentices were nudging each other and pretending to look disgusted. Mr Stokes did not know what to do – it was perhaps the first time this had ever happened to him. The back of his neck reddened like a flame, and he went off to stand with Mr Morgan, at a distance. I raged inwardly at them all, even at the boy, whose name I did not even know. I felt sickened and lost, dropping into a void where there was only misery.

I overheard someone mention the name of the boy. He was Brian Wiltshire. Later on that day, when I was forced to speak to him about a blueprint, he swung round on me like a cornered animal. I had startled him, and I stopped looking into his face. Recovering almost at once, he made himself brash and jaunty.

'How long did you want it for, old boy?' he said, curling his lip.

I was angry with him for treating me as an enemy, lumping me with all the others indiscriminately. Even though I guessed it was not really him, this manner, but only a defence, it made no difference. My sympathy had dwindled.

After about a month I was taken off bench work and put in charge of a small shaping machine. A long greased ram on a crank drove the tool forward slowly, then snatched it back to begin again. It needed dozens of strokes to travel across the piece of metal clamped in the vice. All I needed to do was turn the handles a fraction at a time, in the middle of each stroke, and gaze around me. It was simple, leisurely work.

Mr Morgan wandered round from one group to another, looking bored and glancing at his watch. He sometimes stood by me, pressing up too close, dog-like, until I thought he was doing it for some reason. But his face gave nothing away: I was never certain. He jingled the odds and ends in his pockets and made a pretence of examining my blueprint, hanging his long impudent nose over it. I knew he was not really interested.

Once he asked me, smiling slyly: 'Like it here?'

'Oh yes,' I said in confusion. It was impossible to trust him with the truth.

'Not bad, is it?'

I thought he might be trying to trick me.

'No,' I answered.

'Happy?'

'I think so, yes,' I said, and grinned. It was a kind of game.

'Live anywhere round here?' he asked familiarly, smiling away. I told him.

'No – do you? How d'you get here, then – bus it?'

'On my bike,' I said.

'Really?' he exclaimed, and drew the word out in a cultured drawl. Now and then he affected this. We used to imitate him in the canteen.

'Unless the weather's too bad,' I added.

'Rather you than me,' he smirked. He gave me a waggish prod in the ribs with his elbow. Then he noticed the supervisor beckoning through the glass, so he disowned me. He sprang over to the door, brisk and bustling, suddenly pompous with responsibility.

That Easter I came to the end of my three months' probation. I was called into the glass-walled office and told to report the next day to a section in another part of the factory.

It was very different out there. I was given the oldest lathe, a belt-driven, worn-out thing, and stood among skilled turners in the biggest machine-shop. All around were the intent faces I saw on my first day, and I kept telling myself that this was the adult world I looked at once in nervous fascination, through the wire mesh. It seemed incredible that I should not have realized then how hateful it was. I felt I had been thrown amongst slaves, and because of some terrible obscure fate I was enslaved with them, I should never get away.

The foreman wore a white smock. He spoke in a high, rapid voice, and held his back very straight. Showing me the lathe I was to operate, he consoled me brusquely: 'Don't break your heart over it; this is only temporary. I'll put you on something better in a week or two.' He had misunderstood the expression on my face.

There was nothing difficult about my new job, but I soon found myself in trouble. By the side of my machine was a heap of cast steel bars. They were scaly, brown-coated. I was to get them ready for the skilled men by taking a few rough cuts, removing the tough brown rind; nothing else. The foreman told me not to bother about measurements, and left me to it.

I fastened in the first heavy bar and pushed over the long wooden starting handle. The belt slithered and screeched up near the roof, then gave a final piercing scream and the bar spun round. I daubed on a brushful of suds from the tin can and edged the tool up timidly. It only rubbed. I pressed harder, and burnt the top of the tool. It had made no impression on the tough scale. Discouraged, I took out the tool and went over to the grindstone to resharpen it.

There was a man already using the stone. The wheel roared softly inside its fat casing, which was trembling, as the blurred, rushing edge flung off orange sparks in spasms. It was a very big stone; I was nervous of its size and weight. The thin, crouching man who was there swayed his body sideways before it like a knife-grinder I had seen once when I was a boy. He stopped abruptly, stood up straight and plunged his hot smoking metal into a tray of gritty water. The water hissed and steamed. Then it grew a grey scum.

'Okay,' he said abstractedly, backing away to make room for me.

The surface of the wheel was lumpy. The tool bounced and chattered against it, and I was afraid if I pressed too hard it would wrench out of my hand. I had heard lurid stories of such things, of the tool twisting free and jamming between the tool-rest and the whirling stone, and then the stone cracking, exploding in all directions, the pieces hitting men dozens of yards away.

I was glad to finish. But even with the newly-sharpened tool it was no good. I looked round desperately for the charge-hand, to ask his advice. The foreman stood only a few machines away, but he was too important-looking a person, and I did not want him to know I had failed already. Dick, the charge-hand, was a stout man with tufts of ginger hair round his bald head, who worked in shirt-sleeves and an oily blue pullover. I went looking for him.

'Where you workin'?' he mumbled, staring down at his shoes. He was strangely reserved.

I walked ahead and he half waddled, half rolled after me, throwing out his feet.

He showed me how to grind a better angle on the tool and how to attack the bar with a deep cut, peeling off the scale altogether, the first time. That was the secret, he explained. I wasn't bold enough. I had to listen hard because he talked indistinctly, mouthing and soft, like a shy country man, leaning his woollen belly against the machine. The operation looked so simple now that I wondered what I found so hard. Dick was tightening screws and making various adjustments with a spanner, while his free hand fed the tool into the bar easily, surely. I admired the skill in his puffy red hands.

'Whatever you do, don't nibble at it. Take a good bite,' he mumbled, and went off.

The next morning, as I was about to take a cut, there was a loud crack and the lathe stopped. I looked at it stupidly, baffled. Then the belting dropped from the high shaft, a lifeless snake, and one end struck my shoulder. It was like being hit with a stick. The blood rose in my face and I pursed my lips grimly, suspecting some kind of practical joke for a few seconds.

The belt was broken at the joint. The foreman noticed and shouted across: 'Take it to be mended – he'll bring a ladder back with him. Know where he lives?'

I shook my head, feeling useless, and he pointed over to the far end, upwards. 'See up there, where that kid is? Go as far as the millwrights, and you'll see the stairs.'

Gathering up the dead weight of the belt I was surprised at the length. Where it passed over the pulleys the leather was rubbed smooth and glossy and quite warm. It felt strange to be carrying it away from the place where I worked. I had rolled it up as small as possible, but it was still bulky. I marched down the gangway self-consciously with the thing under my arm.

In the canteen at dinner-time I still sat at the same table with two apprentices from the training centre. I mentioned about the belt breaking, and the steel balcony with a view of everything, where the repairer worked in a cage – a bent old man, in overalls so faded they were nearly white, with a boyish, dirty white mop of hair and a toothless mouth. They knew all about him. 'That's old Sam,' said Robbie, the nearest one, and he made his eyes incredulous, gloating. 'D'you mean to say you didn't know he was up there?'

They had caught me out once more in this game of being 'in the know' which they were always playing. Without managing to answer I pushed more rice pudding into my mouth. It was safer to keep quiet. A wrong reply now would produce a chorus of howls and gibes. There were rules of conversation, even here. Learning to talk like a tough, knowledgeable adult seemed to be part of another slow apprenticeship.

Sitting opposite me was a shrunken little man with a dark monkey face and blackish hands, who arrived later than us and sat down noisily, banging his plate on the table and grunting. He would draw in a huge sigh, spread out his elbows and eat. I have never seen anyone eat the way he did. He would pour a little mountain of salt on the rim of his plate, scoop some up on the end of his knife blade, and let his mouth hang open. The salt was thrown in first, jerkily, and he left his jaw slack so that he could shovel potatoes and cabbage in afterwards with his fork. Then he sat inert, chewing. He was about to pour his hill of salt at this moment. Robbie glanced sideways wildly to attract my attention. I was watching already.

After half an hour there were gaps at many of the tables. A few girls and women would stay, not many, screaming out now and then in laughter, lighting cigarettes. The men left would be split into schools of card players and watchers, and groups where a person talked vehemently and the rest listened, leaning in closely with their heads almost touching. Then there were those belonging to neither, the ones who fell asleep and slept until the first hooter sounded, collapsed on their forearms over the spread newspapers.

Once, towards the end of the dinner hour, I was sitting idly and a youth who had come over to us pushed a sheet of paper at my hands.

'Want to have a look?' he asked, standing near my shoulder.

He was an apprentice, but he didn't work in my bay. I had never seen him before. The paper looked old. It was yellowing, and a lot of different fingers had held it and left marks. Some of the words were badly written and impossible to read. There was about half a foolscap page of it. The vicar's daughter was being taught the facts of life by the narrator. She was innocent but very passionate, and there was no need to seduce her. I read the crude details hastily and handed it back, grinning hotly. Then the hooter burst out wailing, high up on the far wall, above the clock.

We got up with loutish movements and shuffled out through the swing doors and down the steps, separating in the road outside.

Going through the lanes of machines to my section I kept thinking of the grinning, ugly apprentice, who had gaps in his front teeth. That paper was in his pocket, or being passed to someone else. I felt stirred up, excited, and at the same time horribly tainted by what I had read, hating the unknown youth and wanting to read it all again, but in secret, so that I could absorb the details. All afternoon the hot confusion came and went like a rhythm, the mixture of longing and self-disgust.

The weeks passed. I went on skinning the long bars, ploughing off the dark crusts and then dropping each bar of steel down naked in a warm pile on the oil-soaked floor. They looked sleek. The hot metal chips snapped from the nose of the tool, flew into the air smoking, sometimes dropping on my collar or hitting my face. Once a piece shot and clung to my neck and I beat frantically at it to stop the pain.

At last another lathe became vacant and I was moved to that. It had its own motor, and a modern starting handle like the gear lever on a car, near my left hand, which I pulled towards me. I was conscious of my new importance. I did not have to reach over my head to drag across a shaking wooden bar, and nothing squealed when I started up. But I was not used to so much ease. One afternoon, changing some gear wheels to do screw-cutting, I must have leaned against the rubber knob of the starting lever. My hands were among the gears, then the gears moved suddenly and the cogs ripped at the first three fingers of my left hand.

Somebody ran for the foreman. He grabbed my coat from its wire hook on the girder and hurried me down to the surgery. I was white at the lips, the blood dripping freely on the white lines of the gangway.

At the surgery, after a quick consultation, it was decided to rush me down to the hospital.

I sat in the front seat, feeling sick.

'Here's his coat,' the foreman shouted, bundling my jacket through the window. Then we swept out through the gates in the spring afternoon.

At the hospital the driver handed me over to wait my turn with the rest. 'You'll be all right,' he said, and disappeared. I waited an hour, holding my sodden handkerchief round my wounds, and then they dealt with me. I went home on the bus.

As I walked up to the last corner, I saw my mother. She was just about to cross the road and go in.

'Where's your bike?' she asked in amazement, stopping. 'What's happened?'

'They sent me home,' I said, and lifted my damaged hand. The three fingers of fat bandages burned whitely in the dying light. My mother looked blankly at them. I was disappointed.

'What about your bike, will it be safe there – won't somebody take it?' she was asking worriedly, as I followed her into the basement.

I decided to stop being a casualty who was badly shaken. I was getting hungry. Perhaps later on I would be properly appreciated, when the bandages were peeled off and they saw the mess underneath.

As I sat eating, my father came through the door. He strode in cheerfully on his long legs. I had been looking forward to his astonishment.

'Hallo – back early?' he exclaimed, not noticing. His fresh face shone with wonder.

'Look what he's done,' my mother said.

I explained what had happened.

'Did you write your name in the accident-book?' he asked at once.

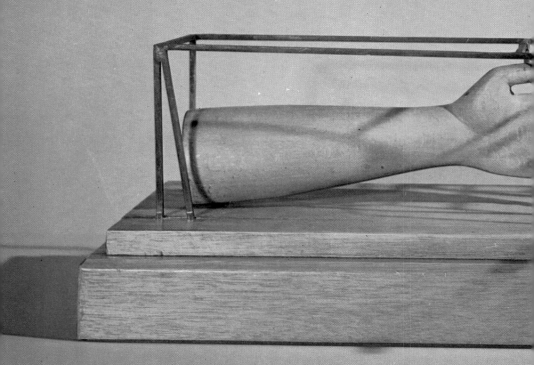

'How could he write in books, like that?' my mother cried.

'I think somebody did,' I said, like a peacemaker.

'You want to make sure,' my father persisted. Nothing made him more stubborn than the idea of justice. 'Cover yourself. It might go septic or something.'

But my hand healed all right, leaving white, rubbery, unwrinkled patches on the backs of my fingers. And there is nothing to see now on two of the fingers. On the third, a strip of newer skin still shows faintly, just below the last joint. No one else would notice. It was seventeen years ago. Looking at it, I remember those days.

PHILIP CALLOW

The Plumber

H. M. BATEMAN

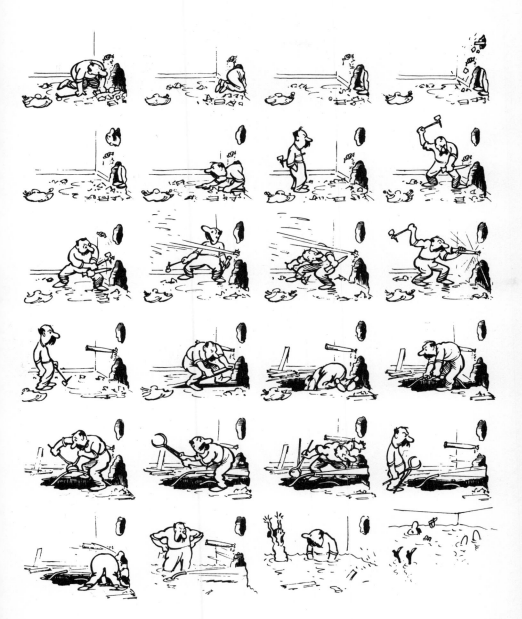

Interview with the Youth Careers Officer

The Youth Careers Office
[The Youth Careers Officer in his cubicle]

OFFICER   Next. *[Enter Harry]* Come into my cubicle. Wait. Signed Arnold Baxter. I am the Youth Careers Officer. Now lad, come on, stand up straight, no slouching, what can I do for you?

HARRY   I want a job.

OFFICER   Oh, just like that, eh? You want a job? Just like that? See all these cards? See them? That's youths wanting jobs. See this handful of cards here, that's jobs.

HARRY   Bad as that, is it? I'll go then.

OFFICER   Oh no you don't! Do me out of a job, would you! Sit down. Card. Had a job before, have you?

HARRY   Yes.

OFFICER   What was it?

HARRY   Paper round.

OFFICER   Good. Good. Paper round is good for a youth. Did you get it through us?

HARRY   No. Through the papers. Situations Vacant columns.

OFFICER   Oh, I see. I see. Situations Vacant. You got it through them? Newspaper columns with the secondhand bikes and the Pets for Miscellaneous Sale. Why didn't you buy a piano while you were about it?

HARRY   Didn't want a piano.

OFFICER   The government goes to all the fuss to build this lovely building, houses us, staffs it with qualified civil servants, we sit here with only two tea breaks a day waiting to serve the public, wanting to serve the public, willing to serve the public and yet you go and get a job through the newspaper columns. Like a lost budgie. But now you come whining to us.

HARRY   You must sit here waiting for a comedian's job to turn up.

OFFICER   Now look, lad. I'm here to help. To serve the public. I'm here to find youths careers. That's why I'm called Youth Careers Officer. I took a course in it. University Sandwich. I was trained in social psychology. I was trained in adolescent problems. So now, button your lip, this is my cubicle. Now, you want a job. What certificates have you got?

HARRY   Certificates?

OFFICER   Mental certificates, lad. Exams. GCE. CSE. DD. Certificates. Qualifications.

HARRY   I've got me Bronze Medallion for Life Saving and me Tenderfoot in the Cubs.

OFFICER   Is that all?

HARRY   Yes.

OFFICER   So, all we need is a job in a forest, by a lake, saving lives. Did you get anything else?

HARRY   No.

OFFICER   What, did they not give you anything when you left?

HARRY   I was supposed to hand me PE kit in, but I kept it.

OFFICER   And that is the sum total of your academic career?

HARRY   Yes.

OFFICER   Well, we could put you to an apprenticeship, on the buildings or in a factory.

HARRY   Apprenticeship is no use. Takes you five years to learn what you could pick up in six months.

OFFICER   You don't want an apprenticeship.

HARRY   No, but I want Saturday afternoons off.

OFFICER   That leaves you with labouring, or semi-skilled.

HARRY   I don't want that.

OFFICER   What sort of thing would you like? Now think about it. I can wait. Take your time. I'm patient. I was trained in psychology and all the rest of it. What sort of job would you like?

HARRY   I would like a job with adventure. Like on the telly. Lots of thrills. Pioneering. Life. Colour. Like the pictures. I was brought up on the pictures.

OFFICER   Would you like to try the Police, you've got the height?

HARRY	I don't like law and order. It usually picks on me. If anything, I would be a cat burglar. But I'm frightened of heights. I keep planning daring daylight robberies but when I get to the stage for shinning up the drainpipe, I can't do it.
OFFICER a model of patience	Well, all we need to find you is a cat-burgling job. Ground floors only. Now, come on, come on, I may have done psychology, but I'm not Job. It'll have to be the last stage of a conveyor belt. You can be the human end of a mechanized system, how will that suit you? Like jam. Take jam. The fruit comes in at one end, and is skinned and stoned by a machine, then it is washed and cleaned in a machine, then it is mixed with sugar in a huge boiler, worked by a machine, then it runs off into jars by a machine process. The jars are lidded by a machine; then they are boxed by a machine, then they are all pushed on conveyor belts and pushed along to the loading bay by a machine; and there on the loading bay is you. Lifting them on to a lorry, the human end to a machine system, how would you like that?
HARRY	Have they got nothing to lift them on with?
OFFICER	The driver likes someone to talk to. Now, I'll fill you in a pink form, look, it's quite personal. It has your number for filing; and I'll put your name on it though that's not really necessary, but it'll make you feel good. Now, run along and present that. Say you're from me, Mr Baxter. They know me down there, I've sent them some good lads. And they keep coming back for more. I'd send my own son down there only the lorry driver wouldn't get on with him.
HARRY	I don't like the idea of a card.
OFFICER	You've got to have a card.
HARRRY	How do I reach the place?
OFFICER	The address is on it, look.
HARRY	But how do I reach it?
OFFICER	Just step outside son, and ask a policeman. Every man to his job.

PETER TERSON *Zigger Zagger*

Proudly, My Son

large, pulpy fruit

The neat little house of mud bricks and galvanized iron, with its battened down blinds of whitewashed hessian, slept peacefully under a canopy of leaning papaw, banana and coconut palms, soughing gently in a breeze from the coast. Moonlight, strong and clear, outlined the windmill, the plot of sweet potato vines and pumpkins, the hard-swept earth round the cottage, with cold clarity.

As the car drew up on the sandy surface of the roadway a chained dog began to bark loudly, savage warning in his throat. A flurry of movement, an outbreak of quick, strained talking as four men hurried through the narrow gateway. In the window a light appeared hesitantly, as kerosene lamps do, burning dully at first then with a hot orange glow. The front door opened.

'Quiet, Shane.' It was a boy's voice. 'Lie down, you fool.' There was a certain rich huskiness in the voice in harmony with the tightly curled head of black hair, the dark hands and face silhouetted by the light behind, the stick-like legs.

From way down the path, the leader of the four men called. 'It's Benson, Phil. I've some friends with me. Wake Digger, will you, son?'

The boy drew aside for them to pass into the house. They saw he was wearing only a pair of shorts washed paper-thin: his torso gleamed smoke-dark and polished, from the tight band of his khaki shorts to the edge of his massed hair. But the mouth was thin-lipped, wide, upturned at the corners, and the bones of the dark face fragile and fine-drawn. Above the flat nose, black eyes set in incredibly bluish whites surveyed them non-committally.

'My father's away with a mob of cattle. Five days longer, perhaps six. He'll come back by way of Tawanga for goods, so –' he spread slim, pink-palmed hands expressively, and shrugged. Benson, who lived on the road out from town could catch him as he passed, the gesture said.

'Oh, God!' The man behind Benson collapsed into a chair, gripping his head despairingly between his two hands. The boy glanced at him with sharper attention. This was Clem Richardson, owner of a part cattle station, part sugar plantation, on the west side of Tawanga. Digger had worked for him.

'A good old bastard,' Digger had called him approvingly. Now his shoulders shook, and the wetness of tears ran through his fingers and over the hairy wrists.

'That's bad, Phil. That's really bad. Made any arrangements for contacting him in an emergency?' Benson had not looked at big Richardson. The other two men stood silent and taut beside him.

The boy shook his head. He turned towards the back of the room, and there, evidently as he'd been aware, stood his mother holding a wrap together in front of her.

'Know how we can reach the old man, Mum?' he asked, though it was clear she'd been following every word said. She came forward when spoken to, nodded briefly to the men, but addressed herself to the boy.

'There's no way until he reaches Rocky. Three days yet, if he's having a good trip. I know the place he stays at in Rocky. They could send a telegram there.'

'Too late! Much too late. By the time he got back here —' Benson stopped abruptly with a shocked glance at big Richardson.

The white woman's eyes darkened. Digger had met her on one of his frequent trips to the outback, a short, stocky, silent woman with a stubborn jaw, daughter of a station hand, with no schooling whatsoever, slow-moving, stoic and spotlessly clean in her habits. They were known to be satisfied with each other. Though Digger, when drunk, was apt to berate her coarsely for not producing more kids: 'That skinny little possum of a Phil – that all you can make out of all my good work?' he would bellow reproachfully. He loved all children with tenderness and understanding, in the way of most aborigines.

'Trouble?' asked the boy, his eyes gliding from one to the other of the strained, haggard faces.

'Clem's girl. Wandered away from the picnic party at Podd's Bay. You know what that country's like, lantana and wattle brush, and the miles of mangrove flats along the tidal creeks.'

The boy showed no surprise. His father was the finest black-tracker in the north, and when a weeping man came to the house at midnight you expected a child – or somebody – to be lost. Sometimes it was animals. A strayed cow of value, a stolen horse, a boar or sow that broke out of its sty and took to the bush. But there were also the sick or aged folk who left their homes for some reason and failed to return, the children who got lost, the husbands or wives who clear out deliberately.

Once, old Fanny White had kidnapped a new-born baby and taken off up-river with it, demented by her longing for a child, nothing more. Digger had found them and brought the baby back none the worse for its sojourn among mosquitoes and its diet of condensed milk.

shrubs

temporary stay

33

greedily, for the
love of money

That time, reflected Phil mercenarily, they'd collected for the
fridge amongst the townspeople and presented it to Digger. He'd
never take payment in cash for tracking, but when they dobbed in
for presentations such as the fridge he accepted them shyly,
abashedly, afterwards running his black fingers over the inscription,
if any, a pleased smile on his heavy, sensual face.

Digger had a superstition about taking money in return for saving
a life, tracking was his personal gift from the Gods, his secret,
mysterious power, his extra-sensory quality. He regarded it as a
sacred trust, convinced that it must be kept as shiningly unspotted
as the barrel of his favourite gun. Money could defile it.

'Bad country,' Phil agreed, 'When was she missed?'

'At midday. We waited a while, thinking she'd turn up. Everybody
cooked their fish, ate, tidied up, yarned and smoked a while. Four
families of us.' He indicated the three other fathers. 'Then somebody said Wanda hadn't returned from her stroll in the bush. I
made a few silly puns on her name and wanderlust – by God, we'll
have to get some conveniences put up at that beach. Remember last
year? A bloke got bit by a brown snake when he –? But then Mrs
Clem started to get anxious. Thinking of snakes again, I suppose.
Clem went for a walk to see if she was coming back – her footprints
were easy to pick up at first in the flat, unmarked sand. About an
hour later he came in looking scared. He'd found she veered off the
trail back to the picnic spot. After a bit the kid must have panicked,
knowing she wasn't going in the right direction. She started to run.
By then she was headed into the lantana and wattle. Clem knew it
was urgent and came back to get help.

'We spent all afternoon searching and calling, figuring she
couldn't have got too far, a little girl like that, only eight – steady,
Clem. We'll find her.'

out of place

Nobody seemed to think it incongruous that a group of men
should explain their every move to a boy. Nobody showed any
restiveness nor impatience with the time it took to give the details.

'You didn't follow the footprints?' The boy's eyes were on his
mother as she set coffee to percolate, her movements sluggish. The
boy and the woman had not spoken again to each other, yet they
communicated by some unseen channel. She was already getting
down the rucksack, packing it with first-aid necessities, apples,
brandy, a thermos ready for filling.

'By then we couldn't see any tracks,' Benson admitted despairingly. 'You know what the ground's like there – sparse grass, inches
deep layer of dead leaves. Once she reached the lantana she never
left a mark to show which way she went.'

The boy shook his head impatiently. 'She left signs all right, if you'd known what to look for. It'll be useless now, after so many people have trampled through the scrub. We'll have to pick it up where she came out, since she's not in the scrub. She'd have been found if she was.'

'Yes. The police are there now, and the neighbours. Must be a hundred, all told, searching.'

The boy pulled a shirt over his head, then a woollen pullover. 'I'm not my old man, of course, ' he admitted. 'But he's taught me a lot. I might be able to help.' He lifted his head with a show of pride. 'I'm his son.'

Clem Richardson raised a despairing face to stare at him wordlessly. Anguished, he waved a rejecting hand. What could this half-caste boy do when searchlights, police, loudspeakers, experienced bushmen, were achieving nothing.

'We've got to get help –' he began vaguely, shaking his head from side to side as if to clear it of terrible visions stamped there. 'It's cold out of doors, surprisingly so for the time of year –' and Wanda dressed only in a brief sunsuit of polka-dotted seersucker! He shuddered.

'Look, Clem, Digger idolizes this kid. He's been all over the country with his father. He must have picked up a lot from Digger.'

'A kid, though! A bloody *kid!*'

The boy passed round cups of coffee, steaming and black. 'Thirteen next July,' he told them with childish pride completely at variance with the calm acceptance of responsibility he'd just shown. It's a funny age, Benson thought with a kind of pity. Neither man nor child, but part one and part the other. 'The old man's giving me a gun – but don't tell Sergeant Yates.'

Nobody said anything. It was improbable they'd even remember what he'd just confided.

Reverting to his role of adult, he went on, 'It won't be daylight for a few hours yet. First thing we gotta find out is where she left the scrub. You gotta have a starting point. If she went down to the river to drink anywhere –' he smiled encouragingly at the unseeing men – 'she will have left tracks even the police can't miss.'

'We'd better go,' big Richardson urged, putting down his scarcely touched cup. . . .

A group of women sat outside a hastily rigged tentfly, clustered together about a dying campfire. They were sleepless, and exhausted by sleeplessness. A kerosene-tin full of water bubbled at the side of the fire, ready for tea-making. From time to time somebody came in and wanted a hot drink, wanted to fill billies with tea and take them back to the searchers.

They had fresh news for the men. Searchers with a spotlight had found where the little girl slid down the river bank, stooped to drink, and then, apparently crossed the river. It was very shallow there at the bend and a popular crossing for driven cattle. Her prints led up the flatter opposite side of the river bank, then petered out.

Dawn tinged the sky with a pink glow which took on a tinge of orange as they set off through the sparse, low-growing coastal shrubs – sarsaparilla, emu-berry, bread-fruit and bottle-brush. Here was a wide, beaten track easy to follow, for many people had passed along it during the day, clearing it of overhanging branches. At first there had been just the imprint of a single row of small foot-steps, now it was ploughed up by many feet.

When they came to the lantana shrubbery it wasn't so easy to walk erect. Lantana scrub grows like a billowing sea, matted, thorny, im-penetrable – but for the cattle pads and wallaby tracks which criss-crossed it. The breakers of this trail must have had a pretty rough time getting through; it was partly beaten down now.

When they reached the bank of the river it was to see a group of thirty or forty men gathered there, some resting, smoking, talking in a desultory way and watching the sky. Others were at work amongst saddled horses, freeing some, haltering others, tightening girths on those ready to start work once more. These too looked up at the sky from time to time, seeing the brilliant dawn with obvious relief. Rain would write a tragic finish to their efforts if it fell now. Not only would it wash out all sign of the child's footmarks but it would add to the tortures of exposure for her. She would die in the rain, almost certainly.

The men, all of them dark with fatigue, beard, dirt and blood from scratches, eyed the boy curiously. They all knew him, and knew his father better. Their own kids had not been allowed to join in the search and it worried them to see the coloured boy there, taking a man's place.

'Couldn't locate Digger?' someone asked dejectedly. The thought that the black-tracker's services were available if the kid wasn't quickly found had buoyed them all up with hope during the long, unrewarding hours.

'Away with cattle.' Benson sat on a log. The sun rose above the mountain range to the east. He glanced at Richardson doubtfully. The man stood looking silently at the vast sweep of empty country, grasstree land, not tall-timbered, not impressive to look at, but stretching relentlessly unaltered for miles. A pitiless breadth of country. Where the river poured into the bay, and cutting a green swath through the brown and olive vegetation, was the brilliant, shimmering, emerald green of mangroves. Even the awakening bird-life added to the macabre atmosphere of the morning. Somewhere in that harsh landscape a little girl listened to the wild singing of a myriad birds; the raucous cries of crows on the hunt, the laughter of kookaburras. Her fear and loneliness must be acute.

In the meantime the boy had been casting about the edges of the camp. Shyly, unobtrusively, for he was a little afraid of all these grim-faced men. Several of them rode away, impatient of relying on a mere kid to show them anything. Some watched him indifferently. Benson's eyes had never roamed far from him, and his gaze was intent. And he saw at once when Phil found what he sought.

'Got a lead, Phil?'

The boy's tongue clove to the roof of his mouth. What had he found, after all? What has a dog found when it follows a beloved master across a teeming city? Nothing tangible. Just a prickling of instinct – a riffling of hyper-sensitive nerve ends – nothing you could define.

Phil had seen a smoother run of ground, a belt of grey-leaved wattles in the distance. Wattle trees just breaking into a froth of dripping gold. He knew the child would go instinctively towards the shelter of the wattles.

'Dunno, Boss.' He had slipped unconsciously into his father's way of addressing white males. He set off in the direction he sensed she had gone, like a pigeon homing.

'He's on to something,' Benson said constrainedly, rising. But it was nearly half a mile away that he found his first proof, endorsement of his own judgement. A small, barely discernible toe-print on a patch of bare earth where something had razed the grass. A print pointing indisputably in the direction he was already headed. His nostrils flared as he took a deep breath. 'She went this way,' he said.

Long past midday they found where she had spent the night. A broken leaf here, a green twig there, seldom as much as a discernible print, held the boy tirelessly to the trail all through the morning's blazing heat. The sun was a ball of fire in a copper sky. The sound of a booming surf on a cement-hard beach far away could be clearly heard in the unstirring lifelessness of the bush.

The men had been, on the whole, unwilling to trust in the boy's ability. So much depended on finding the child quickly. The boy was untried, and after all, only a boy. Only Benson, Richardson and a red-haired man called Parker followed him.

Later in the afternoon a rider caught up with them. Richardson was wanted at the nearest phone. His wife had gone into labour with her fourth child.

He went like a dumb ox, no longer capable of making his own decisions. His tortured mind had found refuge at last in a fog of blankness, for the moment he was insulated from further suffering.

At five o'clock they plainly saw where the child had entered the mangrove swamp. The soft mud held the imprint of her feet like plaster casts. Sandflies and mosquitoes flew in a black cloud about their faces and hands, and Benson began to swell ominously from the stings. He'd been poisoned a year ago by sandflies.

'How could she have come so far – a baby like her – it's incredible!' he said, viciously slapping at his exposed parts with a leafy branch.

As night fell they were out of the swamp again, climbing into foothills and gullies. In the gathering darkness Parker gave a smothered cry and dropped to the ground.

'I'm bit! Look out, you fool – it's in that tussock – what kind is it for God's sake?'

He was already ripping the leg of his trousers upward on the seam. The boy killed the small snake while Benson cut the bite, sucked it, loosened the tourniquet, all very swiftly and without talk of any kind.

The still contorting body of the switch-like snake was closely examined in the dusk. 'Black,' agreed Parker, after they'd all given an opinion. 'Well, I'll have to get back, I suppose.'

'Mr Benson will go with you. I'll carry on here. I'll leave clear markings and you can catch me up again tomorrow.' The last sentence was directed at Benson, whose face had fallen at the idea of being out of things.

'You can manage by yourself, Phil?' he asked heavily, disappointed.

'I can manage, Mr Benson.'

When the two men had gone he hurried on, sure that somewhere just ahead lay the place where she had slept last night. Before night fell altogether he wanted to reach that spot.

The imprint of her body on the broken fronds of fern was where he'd expected to find it, between two huge protecting boulders. There was a little pile of guava seeds she'd spat out whilst eating the acrid fruit, some wild plum stones and a patch of dampness where something containing water had stood. Evidently she'd found an old

cut off

tin near the river and filled it, carrying it with her through the long, hot day. It must leak a little. It wouldn't, he decided, last her long. Next morning she made good time, travelling fast towards the distant sound of booming surf. But she tired early. Her wandering tracks were hard to follow, she seemed to go off at a tangent for no reason. He ate his last meat sandwich, thinking as he looked at the stale white bread in his dark fingers that her life lay now in those same hands. The searchers would never find her in time.

It was worse when she entered the great, never-ending belt of red sandstone. Great flats of reef-like, heat-reflecting stone, with little vegetation, nothing to show which way a terrified, dropping, heat-stricken child would go. Only the blazing red sun throwing back its own intensified rays from that inferno.

But she had crossed it, and she must have left signs somewhere.

persistently | Patiently, inexorably, tirelessly, the boy kept on. And found it again – scarcely more than a breath of disturbed air where the child had passed. Enough to go on – to point the right direction in which his further search lay. Over the mountain ridge now. . . .

He gained the summit as the sun set, a tiny figure silhouetted against the sun's crimson display of grandeur, his lips cracked from thirst and heat but his small head up, as if he scented the breeze for his quarry. His body was tensed and eager in spite of the paralysing fatigue that ached in every limb and muscle.

He was considering. Night was almost upon him once more. The child's third night of exposure. She'd never live to see another if she weren't caught up with soon.

Ahead lay the blankly soaring range of mountains, stony, gutted by late fires, grim as death itself. Surely no child would climb it, *could* climb it? If he made the right decision now he could go straight to her, without waiting to verify every step he took. It was too late, anyway, to work by tracking now. She must be found to-night and just at his back crept the ever-deepening dusk.

He chose the easiest descent he could find, then started down the ridge, grateful for the relaxing of his muscles. He had merely to lean forward: so steep was the side of the ridge that his legs automatically kept moving without effort. Yes, he thought, she is dropping on her feet. She came this way. It is the only way she could keep moving.

The first stars were out, rather faint and flickering, sad stars, he thought. And his legs were still covering the ground with awkward, stumbling steps.

Then he saw it – the bundle of white rags, lying like a heap of feathers under a twisted wild apple tree. Afraid to take his eyes off it

41

for fear it vanished, like a mirage, he shambled up to within a few feet of it. In the light of the torch the child materialized, her face raw with broken blisters, blackened with dirt and sweat, the tangled hair lying fanned out on the bare earth. The spotted playsuit was in shreds. One cruelly burned shoulder showed through a rent in the thin material. The small feet were swollen, torn, filthy. And over every inch of skin erupted the painful, red lumps and scratches of insect bites.

heavily
But she breathed. Stertorously, it is true, but she was alive. She did not stir as he flashed the torch over her, nor yet when he bent close and spoke her name. Touching her hand, he found it fiercely hot, then even as he held it thoughtfully in his own, she began to shiver violently.

Sunstroke, perhaps. A chill. Exhaustion, certainly. There had been no attempt made to find shelter for the forthcoming night.

He turned, studying apprehensively the mountain range he had crossed today. His heart failed him. Thin and almost dehydrated as she appeared, even so, how could he ever carry her up and over that forbidding barrier?

The chill, cutting wind sweeping out of the gorges froze the perspiration on his skin as he bent to lift her across his shoulders. Out on the ranges one dingo howled and was answered by several closer at hand. He began the ascent, wondering almost idly how far he'd get before they both fell. . . . Useless to return the way he had come. To cut across country would cut off miles. And perhaps Benson would catch up some time tomorrow.

At daylight he ran into a group of riders still searching. He scarcely heard the gun signals fired; scarcely felt the child's weight lifted out of his arms. They gave him water and he could just let it trickle down his throat – too tired to swallow. Too tired to talk. Too tired to listen.

Benson drove him home next day in his shiny big Customline. They didn't say much. The boy was watching the man's hairy hands on the slender steering wheel, wishing it belonged to him. It was a super car, all gorgeous cream and scarlet and chrome fittings.

'Clem's a rich man, son. He'll want to make it up to you. He's big-hearted, Clem is.'

The boy shook his head. Benson grinned. 'A birthday present, maybe?'

'Maybe.' Phil smiled too.

'Look here, you don't believe that stuff Digger spouts, about money bringing bad luck to a tracker, do you? You're educated. Your mother's a white woman, and a damned fine one. Don't let that hoodoo yabber influence you, Phil. A boy like you –' he wanted to add: a boy I'd be proud to call my own son. But he couldn't. That was Digger's privilege, to call this thin, heroic kid 'my son'. The boy said nothing. He was watching the speedometer with great interest.

'All right, Phil.' Benson sighed. 'I'll tell Clem. He'll make it good, you can be sure of that.'

When he pulled up at the cottage under the leaning banana trees he saw the boy's mother hoeing corn in the distance, a straw hat tied on her head by means of a red scarf.

The boy was turning to go indoors, but abruptly, suddenly, he turned back, with a·wide grin.

'With an inscription?' he asked eagerly, his eyes dancing with pleasure.

'Sure thing, Dig. With an inscription.'

Perhaps, Phil thought, Mr Benson had forgotten it was only himself he was talking to, not his father. Unless he'd said it on purpose? Wouldn't *that* tickle the old man!

And whistling, he went indoors to look for something more to eat. He was always hungry.

E. A. GOLLSCHEWSKY

The Man who was Shorter than Himself

There was a man two inches shorter than himself
Who always kept getting stuck in the sidewalk;
And when the curious townsmen came
To yank his arms and crush his hat,
He'd spit in the eye of the lean
And steal the wallets off the fat.

KENNETH PATCHEN

Sunset

BLACK DESPERADO SLAIN

The Negro who has terrorized this locality for two days, killing three men, two whites and a Negro, was killed last night with machine-gun fire by detachments of the –th Regiment, State National Guard. The troopers set up their gun before the copse in which the black was hiding, and when there was no reply to their fire, Captain Wallace entered the place and found the Negro dead. No reason has been ascertained for the black's running amuck, though it is believed he was insane. He has not been identified.
The Clarion Eagle

He came part of the way on or in or beneath freight cars, but mostly he walked. It took him two days to come from Carrollton Avenue to Canal Street, because he was afraid of the traffic; and on Canal Street at last, carrying his shotgun and his bundle, he stood frightened and dazed. Pushed and shoved, ridiculed by his own race and cursed by policemen, he did not know what to do save that he must cross the street.

So at last, taking his courage in both hands and shutting his eyes, he dashed blindly across in the middle of the block. Cars were about him, a taxi driver screamed horrid imprecations at him, but, clutching his gun and bundle, he made it. And then a kind white man directed him to the river which he sought.

curses

And here was a boat, all tied up to the bank, waiting for him. In climbing down a pile and leaping six feet of water to get on it, he nearly lost his gun; and then another white man, cursing, drove him from the boat.

'But, cap'n,' he protested, 'I jes wants to go to Af'ica. I kin pay my way.'

'Africa, hell,' said the white man. 'Get to hell off this boat. If you ever try to get on here again that way I'll shoot you. Get on up yonder and get a ticket, if you want to ride.'

'Yes, suh. 'Scuse me, cap'n.'

'What?' repeated the ticket seller in amazement.

'Lemme have a ticket to Af'ica, please um.'

'Do you mean Algiers?'

'No'm; Af'ica.'

'Do you want a ferry ticket?'

'Yassum, I expec' so: so I kin ride dat boat waitin' yonder.'

'Come on, come on, up there,' said a voice from the waiting queue behind him, so he took his ticket and was hustled through the gate and was once more on board the ferry.

To his surprise the boat, instead of going down the river, in which direction he vaguely supposed Africa to be, held straight across the stream, and he was herded ashore like a sheep. Clinging to his gun he stared about him helplessly. At last he diffidently approached a policeman.

'Cap'n, suh, is dis Af'ica?'

'Huh?' said the startled officer.

'Ah'm tryin' to get to Af'ica, please suh. Is dis de right way?'

'Africa, hell,' said this white man, just as the steamboat man had done. 'Look here, what are you up to?'

'Ah wants to go back home, whar de preacher say us come fum.'

'Where do you live, nigger?'

'Back up yonder ways, in de country.'

'What town?'

'Ain't no town, suh, 'ceptin Mis' Bob and de fambly and his niggers.'

'Mississippi or Louisiana?'

'Yessuh, I 'speck so.'

'Well, lemme tell you something. You go back there on the first train you can catch. This ain't no place for you.'

'But, cap'n, I wants to go to Af'ica.'

'You forget about Africa, and go buy yourself the longest railroad ticket you can, do you hear?'

'But cap'n –'

'Beat it now. Do you want me to take you up?'

At the foot of Canal Street again, he looked about him in perplexity. How did one get to Africa? He was hustled and shoved this way and that, and he allowed destiny to carry him along the river front. Here was another boat tied up to the wharf, with niggers carrying things up a plank and dumping them down upon the floor. A coatless white man was evident, loudly.

Niggers pushing trucks rattled and banged, singing, about him. He was still thrust around, leaping from the path of one truck only to find another bearing down upon him. 'Look out, black man!'

Suddenly, the boss whirled upon him.

'What in hell are you doing? Grab ahold of something there, or get off this job. I don't have no spectators on this job at all. You hear me.'

'Yes suh, cap'n,' he returned equably; and soon he was throwing sacks on to a truck. His blood warmed with activity, he began to sweat and to sing. This was where he was at home – for the first time in how long? He had forgotten. 'Af'ica, where is you?' he said.

Quitting time: the sun hung redly in the west and the long

shadows were still and flat, waiting for dark. The spinning golden motes spun lower in the last sunlight; and the other hands gathered up coats and lunch pails and moved away towards the flashing street lights, and supper. He picked up his gun and bundle and went aboard the boat.

Among soft, bulky sacks he lay down to munch the loaf of bread he had bought. Darkness came down completely, the lapping of water against the hull and the pungently sweet smell of the sacked grain corn soon put him to sleep.

Motion waked him, a smooth lift and a steady drumming of engines. Light was about him and he lay in a dullness of comfort, not even thinking. Then he found that he was hungry, and wondering mildly where he was, he got up.

As soon as he appeared on deck another mad white man fell upon him.

'Ah wants to go to Af'ica, cap'n,' he protested, 'when I help dem niggers loadin' yestiddy Ah thought us was all goin' on dis boat.'

The white man bore him down with tides of profanity. 'God in heaven, you niggers will drive me crazy. Don't you know where this boat is going? It's going to Natchez.'

'Dat suit me all right, jes' so she pass Af'ica. You jes' tell me when we gits dar and if she don't stop I kin jump off and swim to de bank.'

The man looked at him for a long minute quite in amazement.

'En don,t worry about de fare neither, suh,' his passenger hastened to reassure him. 'I got money: I kin pay it.'

'How much you got?'

'Plenty, cap'n,' he replied grandly, digging in his overalls. His out-thrust hand held four silver dollars, and some smaller coins. The white man took the four dollars.

'Well, I'll take you as far as Africa for this. And you get on up there and help them niggers shift cargo until we get there.'

'Yas, suh!' he said with alacrity. He paused again. 'But you'll sho' tell me at de right station, won't you, cap'n?'

'Yeh, sure. But beat it now, and help them other boys. G'on now.'

He helped the other boys while they passed under the perfect day from one shimmering reach of the river to another; and again the sun hung redly in the west. Bells rang somewhere and the boat sheered in towards the shore. More bells, the boat lost speed and nosed easily into the mud beneath a row of barrels. The white cap'n, the mad one, leaned down from the front porch above his head.

'All right, Jack,' he roared, 'here you are. Help put them barrels on board, and Africa is about a mile across them fields yonder.'

He stood to watch the boat draw away from the shore, trailing black smoke from its tall funnels across the evening; then he shouldered his gun and struck inland. He had not gone far when he thought of the lions and bears he would probably meet, so he stopped and loaded his gun.

After walking until all the light was gone and the Dipper swung majestically down the west, he knew that he must be well into Africa, and that it was time to eat and sleep again. To eat he could not, so he decided to find a safe place to sleep. Tomorrow he could probably kill a rabbit. He suddenly found a fence beside him; across it loomed something that might be a haystack. He climbed the fence and something rose horribly from almost under his feet.

He knew stark and terrible fear. His gun leaped to his shoulder and roared and flamed in the darkness, and the lion or whatever it was plunged bellowing away into the night. He could feel sweat cold as copper plates on his face and he ran towards the haystack and clawed madly at it, trying to climb it. His fear grew with his futile efforts, then cooled away, allowing him to mount the slippery thing. Once on top he felt safe, but he was cautious to place the shot-gun close to his hand as he lay on his belly, staring into the night. The thing he had shot was quiet now, but the night was filled with sounds.

A light came twinkling along the ground and soon he could see legs criss-crossed it and he heard voices in a language he could not understand. Savages, he thought, folks that eat you; and he crouched lower in his straw. The light and the voices passed on in the direction the beast he had shot had taken; soon the light stopped beside a blotched thing that swelled up from the ground, and the voices rose in imprecation.

'Gentlemen!' he breathed. 'I mus' a shot dem folks' own private lion.'

But a lion was a lion. And so he lay hidden while the light moved on away and was lost at last, and the stars swung over him and he slept.

He was shaken into wakefulness. He threw an arm across his eyes. That strange language was in his ears again and he opened his eyes to see a small dark-skinned man kneeling over him with a pistol. The language he could not understand, but the language the pistol talked he could.

They are going to eat me! he thought. His leg gathered and sickled, the man toppled backward towards the ground and as an animal leaps he flung himself bodily earthward. A pistol went off and something slapped him dully in the shoulder. He replied, and a man flopped to the ground. He leaped to his feet and ran, while bullets whined past him. The fence was before him: he turned to follow it, seeking a gate.

His left arm was warm and wet, and there at the turn of the fence was a gate. The shooting behind him continued, he clutched his own gun as he saw a running figure, trying to cut him off at the gate. As they drew together he saw that this one was a member of his own race. 'Out de way, nigger,' he gasped at the other's waving arms; and he saw the expression of ludicrous amazement on the man's face as his gun crashed again.

His breath came in gulping lungsful. He must stop. Here was a ditch, and a long embankment. Just ahead, where another embankment intersected it, was a small copse. Into this he plunged, concealed, and lay on his back, panting. His heaving lungs at last breathed easier. Then he discovered the wound in his shoulder. He looked at his blood in surprise. 'Now when you suppose dat happen?' he thought. 'Whew! Dese Af'ikins shoots niggers jes' like white folks does.'

He bound it crudely, then took stock of the situation. He had shelter and that was all. There were still eighteen shells left. And he would need them: there was already one man about two hundred yards away, holding a rifle and watching his thicket. 'Don't ack like he gwine bother me right soon,' he decided. 'I'll jes' rest here twell dark, and den I'm gwine back to Mist' Bob. Af'ica sho' ain't no place fer civilized folks – steppin' on lions, and being shot, and havin' to shoot folks yo'self. But I guess dese Af'icans is used to it.'

His shoulder begun to throb dully. He twisted and turned in his mounting fever. How thirsty he was! He had been hungry, but now he was only thirsty, and he thought of the cool brown creek at home, and the cold spring in the wood lot. He raised his sweating face and saw the watchman had drawn closer in. He raised his gun, aiming the best he could with one hand, and fired. The watchman fell backward, leaped to his feet and ran dodging beyond range. 'Jes' to skeer you,' he muttered.

Things were beginning to look funny, and his shoulder hurt dreadfully. He dozed a moment and thought he was at home again: he waked to pain and dozed again. Dozing and waking, he passed the long day, crawling at intervals to sip the muddy, stinking water in the ditch. At last he waked to night, and lanterns and fires and men walking in the firelight and talking.

He had dragged himself down the bank for water, and as he returned an automobile's lights were suddenly turned full on him. A voice screamed and bullets whipped about him. He plunged back to his copse and fired blindly at the light. A man shrieked and bullets ripped and tore at the thicket: the limbs were whipped as by a gale, tortured against the sky. He was seared as with hot irons, and he lowered his head, pressing his face into the muddy earth.

The firing suddenly ceased; the silence literally dragged him from the regions of oblivion. He thrust his gun forward, waiting. At last the darkness detached itself and became two things; and in the flash of his point-blank explosion he saw two men crouching. One of them fired a pistol almost in his face, and fled.

Again it was dawn. The sun rose, became hot, and marched above his head. He was at home, working in the fields; he was asleep, fighting his way from out a nightmare; he was a child again – no, he was a bird, a big one like a buzzard, drawing endless black circles on a blue sky.

Again the sun sank. The west was like blood: it was his own blood painted on to a wall. Supper in the pot, and night where there were no fires and people moving around them, and then all stopping as though they were waiting for something to happen.

He raised his face from the mud and looked at the circle of fires about him. It looked as though everybody had gathered at one place directly in front of him, all watching or waiting for something. Let them wait: tomorrow he'll be at home, with Mr Bob to curse him in his gentle voice, and regular folks to work and laugh and talk with.

Here was a wind coming up: the branches and bushes about him whipped suddenly to a gale fiercer than any yet; flattened and screamed and melted away under it. And he, too, was a tree caught in that same wind: he felt the dull blows of it, and the rivening of himself into tattered and broken leaves.

The gale died away, and all broken things were still. His black, kind, dull, once-cheerful face was turned up to the sky and the cold, cold stars. Africa or Louisiana: what care they?

WILLIAM FAULKNER

The Pious Lion

There was a man walking in the jungle, I don't know if he was a missionary or an explorer, but, at any rate, he had no gun with him. Suddenly he met a lion face to face. He knew that if he turned to run, the lion would be on him in a minute, and he had heard that if you stared hard at an animal it would grow uneasy and slink away. So he fixed the lion with his eye. He stared at the lion and the lion stared at him, and so they stood for about five minutes. Then the lion put its paws close together on the ground, and bent its head right down over them. This seemed a bit more hopeful, but the man was pretty nearly hypnotized by this time, and he thought the best thing he could do was to imitate the lion. So he bent his head down over his hands. So they stood for another five minutes.

Then the lion lifted its head and said, 'I don't know what you're doing, but I'm saying grace.'

TRADITIONAL

The Huge Footprint

There is also a more circumstantial account of an adventure which is supposed to have occurred to a Russian hunter in 1918. He told his story in 1920 to L. Gallon, who was then *chargé d'affaires* at the French Consulate at Vladivostok. The hunter was a tall, elderly man, with very bright eyes, white beard and hair, and a tanned face seamed with scars. The French diplomat invited him to lunch, during which he told the following extraordinary tale.

swampy forest

The second year that I was exploring the taiga, I was very much struck to notice tracks of a huge animal, I say huge tracks, for they were a long way larger than any of those I had often seen of animals I knew well. It was autumn. There had been a few big snowstorms, followed by heavy rain. It wasn't freezing yet, the snow had melted, and there were thick layers of mud in the clearings. It was in one of these big clearings, partly taken up by a lake, that I was staggered to see a large footprint pressed deep into the mud. It must have been about two feet across the widest part and about eighteen inches the

footprint

other way, that's to say the spoor wasn't round but oval. There were four tracks, the tracks of four feet, the first two about twelve feet from the second pair, which were a little bigger in size. Then the track suddenly turned east and went into the forest of middling-sized elms. Where it went in I saw a huge heap of dung; I had a good look at it and saw it was made up of vegetable matter.

Some ten feet up, just where the animal had gone into the forest, I saw a sort of row of broken branches, made, I don't doubt, by the monster's enormous head as it forced its way into the place where it had decided to go, regardless of what was in its path.

I followed the track for days and days. Sometimes I could see where the animal had stopped in some grassy clearing and then had gone on forever eastward.

Then, one day, I saw another track, almost exactly the same. It came from the north and crossed the first one. It looked to me from the way they had trampled about all over the place for several hundred yards, as if they had been excited or upset at their meeting. Then the two animals set out marching eastward, one following some twenty yards behind the other, both tracks mingling and ploughing up the earth together.

I followed them for days and days thinking that perhaps I should never see them, and also a bit afraid, for indeed I didn't feel I was big enough to face such beasts alone.

He had a good hunting gun, which would take ball as well as shot, but he had only five cartridges loaded with ball left. All the same he followed the trail as fast as he could, and thought from the freshness of the tracks that he was gaining on the beasts. Meanwhile it was growing bitterly cold, and he had no way of getting warm in the evening except by drinking scalding tea and building a sort of tent of leaves and branches each night.

One afternoon (he went on) it was clear enough from the tracks that the animals weren't far off. The wind was in my face, which was good for approaching them without them knowing I was there. All of a sudden I saw one of the animals quite clearly, and now I must admit I really was afraid. It had stopped among some young saplings. It was a huge elephant with big white tusks, very curved; it was a dark chocolate colour as far as I could see. It had fairly long hair on the hindquarters, but it seemed shorter on the front. I must say I had no idea that there were such big elephants. It had huge legs and moved very slowly. I've only seen elephants in pictures, but I must say that even from this distance (we were some three hundred yards apart) I could never have believed any beasts could be so big. The second beast was around, I saw it only a few times among the trees: it seemed to be the same size.

All this time he had been hiding behind a big larch. When evening came he reluctantly left his point of vantage, because he could no longer bear the cold. Next morning when he returned the beasts had gone. Winter had set in and the weather was too bitter for him to go on tracking them. 'Such,' Gallon remarks, 'was the tale of this man who was too ignorant to know that what he had actually seen were mammoths.'

BERNARD HEUVELMANS

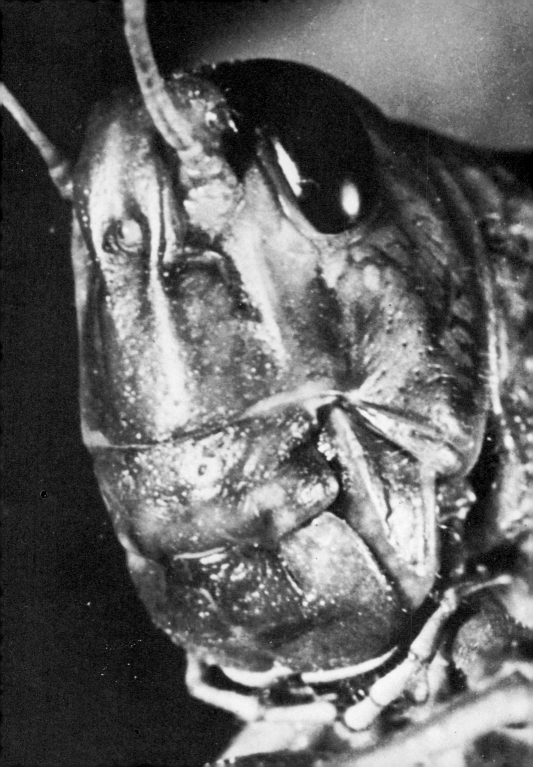

A Mild Attack of Locusts

The rains that year were good, they were coming nicely just as the crops needed them – or so Margaret gathered when the men said they were not too bad. She never had an opinion of her own on matters like the weather, because even to know about what seems a simple thing like the weather needs experience. Which Margaret had not got. The men were Richard her husband, and old Stephen, Richard's father, a farmer from way back, and these two might argue for hours whether the rains were ruinous, or just ordinarily exasperating. Margaret had been on the farm three years. She still did not understand how they did not go bankrupt altogether, when the men never had a good word for the weather, or the soil, or the Government. But she was getting to learn the language. Farmer's language. And they neither went bankrupt nor got very rich. They jogged along, doing comfortably.

Their crop was maize. Their farm was three thousand acres on the ridges that rise up towards the Zambesi escarpment, high, dry windswept country, cold and dusty in winter, but now, being the wet season, steamy with the heat rising in wet soft waves off miles of green foliage. Beautiful it was, with the sky blue and brilliant halls of air, and the bright green folds and hollows of country beneath, and the mountains lying sharp and bare twenty miles off across the rivers. The sky made her eyes ache, she was not used to it. One does not look so much at the sky in the city she came from. So that evening when Richard said: 'The Government is sending out warnings that locusts are expected, coming down from the breeding grounds up north,' her instinct was to look about her at the trees. Insects – swarms of them – horrible! But Richard and the old man had raised their eyes and were looking up over the mountain. 'We haven't had locusts in seven years,' they said. 'They go in cycles, locusts do.' And then: 'There goes our crop for this season!'

But they went on with the work of the farm just as usual, until one day they were coming up the road to the homestead for the midday break, when old Stephen stopped, raised his finger and pointed: 'Look, look, there they are!'

Out ran Margaret to join them, looking at the hills. Out came the servants from the kitchen. They all stood and gazed. Over the rocky levels of the mountain was a streak of rust-coloured air. Locusts. There they came.

At once Richard shouted at the cook-boy. Old Stephen yelled at the house-boy. The cook-boy ran to beat the old ploughshare hanging from a tree-branch, which was used to summon the labourers at moments of crisis. The house-boy ran off to the store to collect tin cans, any old bit of metal. The farm was ringing with the clamour of the gong, and they could see the labourers come pouring out of the compound, pointing at the hills and shouting excitedly. Soon they had all come up to the house, and Richard and old Stephen were giving them orders – Hurry, hurry, hurry.

And off they ran again, the two white men with them, and in a few minutes Margaret could see the smoke of fires rising from all around the farm-lands. Piles of wood and grass had been prepared there. There were seven patches of bared soil, yellow and ox-blood colour, and pink, where the new mealies were just showing, making a film of bright green, and round each drifted up thick clouds of smoke. They were throwing wet leaves on to the fires now, to make it acrid and black. Margaret was watching the hills. Now there was a long low cloud advancing, rust-colour still, swelling forward and out as she looked. The telephone was ringing. Neighbours – quick, quick, there come the locusts. Old Smith had had his crop eaten to the ground. Quick, get your fires started. For of course, while every farmer hoped the locusts would overlook his farm and go on to the next, it was only fair to warn each other, one must play fair. Every-where, fifty miles over the countryside, the smoke was rising from myriads of fires. Margaret answered the telephone calls, and between stood watching the locusts. The air was darkening. A strange darkness, for the sun was blazing – it was like the darkness of a veld fire, when the air gets thick with smoke. The sunlight comes down distorted, a thick hot orange. Oppressive it was, too, with the heaviness of a storm. The locusts were coming fast. Now half the sky was darkened. Behind the reddish veils in front, which were the advance guards of the swarm, the main swarm showed in dense black cloud, reaching almost to the sun itself.

Margaret was wondering what she could do to help. She did not know. Then up came old Stephen from the lands. 'We're finished, Margaret, finished! Those beggars can eat every leaf and blade off the farm in half an hour! And it is only early afternoon – if we can make enough smoke, make enough noise till the sun goes down, they'll settle somewhere else perhaps. . . .' And then: 'Get the kettle going. It's thirsty work, this.'

So Margaret went to the kitchen, and stoked up the fire, and boiled the water. Now, on the tin roof of the kitchen she could hear the thuds and bangs of falling locusts, or a scratching slither as one skidded down. Here were the first of them. From down on the lands came the beating and banging and clanging of a hundred petrol tins and bits of metal. Stephen impatiently waited while one petrol tin was filled with tea, hot, sweet and orange-coloured, and the other with water. In the meantime, he told Margaret about how twenty years back he was eaten out, made bankrupt by the locust armies. And then, still talking, he hoisted up the petrol cans, one in each hand, by the wood pieces set cornerwise across each, and jogged off down to the road to the thirsty labourers. By now the locusts were falling like hail on to the roof of the kitchen. It sounded like a heavy storm. Margaret looked out and saw the air dark with a criss-cross of the insects, and she set her teeth and ran out into it – what the men could do, she could. Overhead the air was thick, locusts everywhere. The locusts were flopping against her, and she brushed them off, heavy red-brown creatures, looking at her with their beady old-men's eyes while they clung with hard serrated legs. She held her breath with disgust and ran through into the house. There it was even more like being in a heavy storm. The iron roof was reverberating, and the clamour of iron from the lands was like thunder. Looking out, all the trees were queer and still, clotted with insects, their boughs weighed to the ground. The earth seemed to be moving, locusts crawling everywhere, she could not see the lands at all, so thick was the swarm. Towards the mountains it was like looking into driving rain – even as she watched the sun was blotted out with a fresh onrush of them. It was a half-night, a perverted blackness. Then came a sharp crack from the bush – a branch had snapped off. Then another. A tree down the slope leaned over, and settled heavily to the ground. Through the hail of insects a man came running. More tea, more water was needed. She supplied them. She kept the fires stoked and filled tins with liquid, and then it was four in the afternoon, and the locusts had been pouring across overhead for a couple of hours. Up came old Stephen again, crunching locusts underfoot with every step, locusts clinging all over him, cursing and swearing, banging with his old hat at the air. At the doorway he stopped briefly, hastily pulling at the clinging insects and throwing them off, then he plunged into the locust-free living-room.

'All the crops finished. Nothing left,' he said.

But the gongs were still beating, the men still shouting, and Margaret asked: 'Why do you go on with it, then?'

'The main swarm isn't settling. They are heavy with eggs. They are looking for a place to settle and lay. If we can stop the main body settling on our farm, that's everything. If they get a chance to lay their eggs, we are going to have everything eaten flat with hoppers later on.' He picked a stray locust off his shirt, and split it down with his thumb-nail – it was clotted inside with eggs. 'Imagine that multiplied by millions. You ever seen a hopper swarm on the march? Well, you're lucky.'

Margaret thought an adult swarm was bad enough. Outside now the light on the earth was a pale thin yellow, clotted with moving shadow, the clouds of moving insects thickened and lightened like driving rain. Old Stephen said: 'They've got the wind behind them, that's something.'

'Is it very bad?' asked Margaret fearfully, and the old man said emphatically: 'We're finished. This swarm may pass over, but once they've started, they'll be coming down from the north now one after another. And then there are the hoppers – it might go on for two or three years.'

Margaret sat down helplessly, and thought: 'Well, if it's the end, it's the end. What now? We'll all three have to go back to town. . . .' But at this she took a quick look at Stephen, the old man who had farmed forty years in this country, been bankrupt twice, and she knew nothing would make him go and become a clerk in the city. Yet her heart ached for him, he looked so tired, the worry-lines deep from nose to mouth. Poor old man. . . . He had lifted up a locust that had got itself somehow into his pocket, holding it in the air by one leg. 'You've got the strength of a steel-spring in those legs of yours,' he was telling the locust, good-humouredly. Then, although he had been fighting locusts, squashing locusts, yelling at locusts, sweeping them in great mounds into the fires to burn for the last three hours, nevertheless he took this one to the door, and carefully threw it out to join its fellows as if he would rather not harm a hair of its head. This comforted Margaret, all at once she felt irrationally cheered. She remembered it was not the first time in the last three years the men had announced their final and irremediable ruin.

'Get me a drink, lass,' he then said, and she set the bottle of whisky by him.

In the meantime, out in the pelting storm of insects, her husband was banging the gong, feeding the fires with leaves, the insects clinging to him all over – she shuddered. 'How can you bear to let them touch you?' she asked. He looked at her, disapproving. She felt suitably humble – just as she had when he had first taken a good look at her city self, hair waved and golden, nails red and pointed. Now she was a proper farmer's wife, in sensible shoes and a solid skirt. She might even get to letting locusts settle on her – in time.

Having tossed back a whisky or two, old Stephen went back into the battle, wading now through glistening brown waves of locusts.

Five o'clock. The sun would set in an hour. Then the swarm would settle. It was as thick overhead as ever. The trees were ragged mounds of glistening brown.

Margaret began to cry. It was all so hopeless – if it wasn't a bad season, it was locusts, if it wasn't locusts, it was army-worms or veld fires. Always something. The rustling of the locust armies was like a big forest in the storm, their settling on the roof was like the beating of the rain, the ground was invisible in a sleek brown surging tide – it was like being drowned in locusts, submerged by the loathsome brown flood. It seemed as if the roof might sink in under the weight of them, as if the door might give in under their pressure and these rooms fill with them – and it was getting so dark . . . she looked up. The air was thinner, gaps of blue showed in the dark moving clouds. The blue spaces were cold and thin: the sun must be setting. Through the fog of insects she saw figures approaching. First old Stephen, marching bravely along, then her husband, drawn and haggard with weariness. Behind them the servants. All were crawling all over with insects. The sound of the gongs had stopped. She could hear nothing but the ceaseless rustle of a myriad wings.

The two men slapped off the insects and came in.

'Well,' said Richard, kissing her on the cheek, 'the main swarm has gone over.'

'For the Lord's sake,' said Margaret angrily, still half-crying, 'what's here is bad enough, isn't it?' For although the evening air was no longer black and thick, but a clear blue, with a pattern of insects whizzing this way and that across it, everything else – trees, buildings, bushes, earth, was gone under the moving brown masses.

'If it doesn't rain in the night and keep them here – if it doesn't rain and weight them down with water, they'll be off in the morning at sunrise.'

'We're bound to have some hoppers. But not the main swarm, that's something.'

Margaret roused herself, wiped her eyes, pretended she had not been crying, and fetched them some supper, for the servants were too exhausted to move. She sent them down to the compound to rest.

She served the supper and sat listening. There is not one maize-plant left, she heard. Not one. The men would get the planters out the moment the locusts had gone. They must start all over again.

'But what's the use of that?' Margaret wondered, if the whole farm was going to be crawling with hoppers? But she listened while they discussed the new Government pamphlet which said how to defeat the hoppers. You must have men out all the time moving over the farm to watch for movement in the grass. When you find a patch of hoppers, small lively black things, like crickets, then you dig trenches around the patch, or spray them with poison from pumps supplied by the Government. The Government wanted them to co-operate in a world plan for eliminating this plague for ever. You should attack locusts at the source. Hoppers, in short. The men were talking as if they were planning a war, and Margaret listened, amazed.

In the night it was quiet, no sign of the settled armies outside, except sometimes a branch snapped, or a tree could be heard crashing down.

Margaret slept badly in the bed beside Richard, who was sleeping like the dead, exhausted with the afternoon's fight. In the morning she woke to yellow sunshine lying across the bed, clear sunshine, with an occasional blotch of shadow moving over it. She went to the window. Old Stephen was ahead of her. There he stood outside, gazing down over the bush. And she gazed, astounded – and entranced, much against her will. For it looked as if every tree, every bush, all the earth, were lit with pale flames. The locusts were fanning their wings to free them of the night dews. There was a shimmer of red-tinged gold light everywhere.

She went out to join the old man, stepping carefully among the insects. They stood and watched. Overhead the sky was blue, blue and clear.

'Pretty,' said old Stephen, with satisfaction.

Well, thought Margaret, we may be ruined, we may be bankrupt, but not everyone has seen an army of locusts fanning their wings at dawn.

Over the slopes, in the distance, a faint red smear showed in the sky, thickened and spread. 'There they go,' said old Stephen. 'There goes the main army, off south.'

And now from the trees, from the earth all round them, the locusts were taking wing. They were like small aircraft, manœuvring for the take-off, trying their wings to see if they were dry enough. Off they went. A reddish brown steam was rising off the miles of bush, off the lands, the earth. Again the sunlight darkened.

And as the clotted branches lifted, the weight on them lightening, there was nothing but the black spines of branches, trees. No green left, nothing. All morning they watched, the three of them, as the brown crust thinned and broke and dissolved, flying up to mass with the main army, now a brownish-red smear in the southern sky. The lands which had been filmed with green, the new tender mealieplants, were stark and bare. All the trees stripped. A devastated landscape. No green, no green anywhere.

By midday the reddish cloud had gone. Only an occasional locust flopped down. On the ground were the corpses and the wounded. The African labourers were sweeping these up with branches and collecting them in tins.

'Ever eaten sun-dried locust?' asked old Stephen. 'That time twenty years ago, when I went broke, I lived on mealie-meal and dried locusts for three months. They aren't bad at all, rather like smoked fish, if you come to think of it.'

But Margaret preferred not even to think of it.

After the midday meal the men went off to the lands. Everything was to be replanted. With a bit of luck another swarm would not come travelling down just this way. But they hoped it would rain very soon, to spring some new grass, because the cattle would die otherwise – there was not a blade of grass left on the farm. As for Margaret, she was trying to get used to the idea of three or four years of locusts. Locusts were going to be like bad weather, from now on, always imminent. She felt like a survivor after war – if this devastated and mangled countryside was not ruin, well, what then was ruin?

But the men ate their supper with good appetites.

'It could have been worse,' was what they said. 'It could be much worse.'

DORIS LESSING

First Frost

A girl is freezing in a telephone booth,
huddled in her flimsy coat,
her face stained by tears
and smeared with lipstick.

She breathes on her thin little fingers.
Fingers like ice. Glass beads in her ears.

She has to beat her way back alone
down the icy street.

First Frost. A beginning of losses.
The first frost of telephone phrases.

It is the start of winter glittering on her cheek,
the first frost of having been hurt.

ANDREI VOZNESENSKY *translated from the Russian by Stanley Kunitz*

The Saturday Dance

DORIS   You don't jive then?

STAN   No, I don't jive.

DORIS   Makes you feel a bit soft.

STAN   What does?

DORIS   When everybody else is jiving,
and you doing slow, slow,
quick, quick, slow.

STAN   Well, you're not forced to jive.

DORIS   You feel so soft.

STAN   There's no law saying you've
got to jive.

DORIS   I know that, but . . .

STAN   I mean, there's no notices up
saying 'Thou shalt jive.'
[Pause]

DORIS   When you asked me for the dance
I thought you meant jiving. . . .

STAN   Oh, all right then, if you don't
like it, we'll pack it in. I'm
sorry you've been troubled.

DORIS   Well, you feel so soft. . . .
[Pause]

STAN   Would you like a cup of coffee or
something?

DORIS   I'll have to look for Mandy.

STAN   Oh aye, that's right, you're with
your friend.

DORIS   There she is, yoo-hoo, Mandy!
there, she's seen me.

STAN   Oh, that's Mandy.

DORIS   Bonny, isn't she? Real shy,
you know. . . .

STAN   Well, I'll be off then. Thank you
for the dance. . . .

DORIS   Hello, love . . . hey, I thought you
were taking us for a cup
of coffee. . . .

STAN   I've just remembered . . . telephone
call I've got to make, sorry. I'll see
you later on, maybe. . . .

DORIS   Well! You meet some funny
types here . . . are you having
a good time, Mandy?
[She moves off in search of better company]

STAN   It's no good, Jack, you shouldn't
have made me come.
[Mimicking] Don't you jive then?

JACK   *[Inner voice]* Well, don't you?

STAN   Not when I've been supping. Makes it swill about too much. Nice gentle waltz, something like that, that's more like it. Oh, hell, it's Latin-American now, that's no good. . . .

JACK   Can't you do that, either?

STAN   Heck, don't you remember that time I did the samba, that time I fell over. You know, that rugby union club dance, when we got chucked out for laughing at the band.

JACK   Yes, I remember. But it's no time for reminiscences. You want to be getting yourself organized. Have a look round, see what sort of a field we've got.

STAN   There's plenty of time.

JACK   Is there heck as like! You know what happens. Old Hotlips Ferguson announces the next dance, and by the time you wake up all the best stuff's gone. You get stuck with the fat ones, the faded ones and them with glasses.

STAN   Like Mandy.

JACK   Yes, like Mandy. Get doing some research. Now, let's see. What about that little blonde piece there, dancing with the bloke in the wedding suit?

STAN   He looks a bit old for her.

JACK   It's Harry Potter, runs the beginners' class on Mondays. He'll be trying to sign her on for the formation dancing team.

STAN   Or something.

JACK   Or something.

STAN   Yes, she's all right.

JACK   Well, try to work up a bit of enthusiasm. She's all right. She's more than all right. She's got a bit of class.

STAN   What if *she's* with a friend?

JACK   Now look. When the music stops, don't let her out of your sight. Then when they announce the next dance, pounce. Don't mess about.

STAN   He's asking her something, look.

JACK   You're all right, she's shaking her head.

STAN   Maybe she doesn't like formation dancing.

JACK   OK. We'll just go over the drill again. What's the first thing you do?

STAN   Get her talking.

JACK   What about?

STAN   About herself.

JACK   Right. Women all like talking about themselves. Find out where she works, then you know where to ring up. What else?

STAN   *[A little wearily]* Don't let her get away. Take her for a cup of coffee.

JACK   It's not very original, but it works. Now, watchit, he's going to announce the next dance. Shirt collar undone, tie dangling, check?

STAN   Check.

JACK   Good lad.

STAN   Have I to do my hollow cheeks?

JACK   Yes, you do that.

STAN   Blast! It's a lady's desire. . . .

JACK   That doesn't matter, ask her to desire you, go on, she's just down there near the next pillar, don't mess about. . . .

STAN   Is it all right though?

JACK   Get on with it, you're wasting time. . . .
       [Pause]

STAN   Excuse me, I wonder if you'd like to desire me. . . .

EILEEN Oh, my feet are ever so tired. . . .

STAN   Are they? Er . . .

JACK   Improvise, improvise. . . .

STAN   I only dance very slowly.

EILEEN All right then.
       [They dance to a waltz tune]

STAN   It's . . . er . . . crowded then.

EILEEN Yes.

STAN   Suppose it's with it being Saturday . . . and that.

EILEEN I expect so.

STAN	Long time since I've been here, don't really like it very much.
EILEEN	Don't you?
STAN	Gets a bit crowded.
EILEEN	Suppose it's with it being Saturday.
STAN	Yes. Yes, I suppose that's it. *[Pause]*
JACK	You're breaking every rule in the book, Stan.
STAN	Oh, button it, can't you?
JACK	Well stop messing about. *[Pause]*
STAN	What's your name then?
EILEEN	Eileen.
STAN	Oh aye. Er . . . nice name. Do you work? I mean, where do you work?
EILEEN	Cracker works.
STAN	You what?
EILEEN	Cracker works.
STAN	Don't think I've heard of that.
EILEEN	It's a big place.
STAN	Yes, yes, I expect it is.
EILEEN	*[Suddenly forthcoming, suggesting she's been weighing Stan up]* They make cream crackers and cheese biscuits and them nylon buns for slimming with.
STAN	Yes, my mum likes them. What do you do then?
EILEEN	Me?
STAN	Yes, what do you do? Butter them?
EILEEN	*[Laughing]* No. I'm a private secretary.
STAN	What, like a typist, you mean?
EILEEN	No, a secretary.
STAN	What's the difference, then? I've often wondered.
EILEEN	I don't know. It just says so on my card.

STAN   Do you like it then?

EILEEN   It's not bad. Money's all right.
[Pause]

JACK   Hold hard, Stan.

STAN   Why?

JACK   That's enough about her for the moment. If she's going to bite, she'll ask about you.

STAN   Will she?

JACK   Nice touch about buttering the biscuits. Always helps if you can get a laugh. Breaks the tension.

STAN   Thank you. I'll wait then.
[Pause]

EILEEN   What's your name then?

STAN   *[Without thinking]* Funny you should say that. He said you might. . . .

EILEEN   What you talking about?

STAN   Sorry. I was thinking about something else. Er . . . Stan, Stanley for short, no, the other way about.
[He is a little nervous]

EILEEN   What's the matter?

STAN   Nothing. Just call me Stan.

EILEEN   I suppose I ought to ask you where you work, if we're being polite and that.
[She knows the rules]

STAN   I'm just a clerk. Sort of low-class civil servant.

EILEEN   Where? Up at the Town Hall?

STAN   Down the Labour Exchange.

EILEEN   Do you like it?

STAN   It's lousy.

EILEEN   Oh.
[Pause]

JACK   You big nit! Saying a thing like that.

STAN   It is lousy.

JACK   You don't have to tell the flaming truth. She doesn't know what to say now.

STAN   Sorry, Jack.

JACK   You're getting cocky with it, that's the trouble. You'd better try to sort it out.
         [Pause]

STAN   Mind you, we have some good fun in the office, it's just the paper-work gets a bit much sometimes.

EILEEN   What sort of fun?

STAN   Well, see, we all have a counter to look after. There's Sid on Heavy Industrial, George on Engineering, Herbert on Clerical, me on Miscellaneous. With me being the youngest, I've only been there two months, I get Miscellaneous, you see. Well, we have these competitions to see who can get the longest queue. Blimey, it's a laugh.

EILEEN   You mean the men just stand there and you don't bother with them?

STAN   They'll stand there for hours sometimes, and not a dickey-bird. Old Sid's the best of the lot, you ought to see the queues he gets. . . .

EILEEN   Well I don't think that's very funny.

STAN   Don't you?

EILEEN   I bet the men in the queue don't laugh.

STAN   That's all right, they're only . . . come to think of it, they don't.

EILEEN   I think it's rotten.

STAN   Well we don't actually do it as much as we used to . . . [Trying to retrieve the situation] It was Sid's idea, he's a bit twisted, is Sid.

EILEEN   He must be.

STAN   Yes, he is . . . er, would you like a cup of coffee?

EILEEN   I don't know.

STAN   What do you mean you don't know?

EILEEN   It's a bit difficult.

STAN   It's all right, I'll pay.

EILEEN   Do you mind waiting five minutes?

STAN   Five minutes? No, I don't think. . . .

EILEEN   Well wait at the bottom of the stairs, you know where I mean, and if I don't come in five minutes I'm not coming OK?

STAN   All right. That is, it's all right as long as you come.

EILEEN   *[Coy]* Well, that's up to you, isn't it?
[She moves away]

ALAN PLATER *The Mating Season*

You Should have Seen the Mess

I am now more than glad that I did not pass into the Grammar School five years ago, although it was a disappointment at the time. I was always good at English, but not so good at the other subjects!!

I am glad that I went to the Secondary Modern School, because it was only constructed the year before. Therefore, it was much more hygienic than the Grammar School. The Secondary Modern was light and airy, and the walls were painted with a bright, washable gloss. One day, I was sent over to the Grammar School, with a note for one of the teachers, and you should have seen the mess! The corridors were dusty, and I saw dust on the window ledges, which were chipped. I saw into one of the classrooms. It was very untidy in there.

I am also glad that I did not go to the Grammar School, because of what it does to one's habits. This may appear to be a strange remark, at first sight. It is a good thing to have an education behind you, and I do not believe in ignorance, but I have had certain experiences, with educated people, since going out into the world.

I am seventeen years of age, and left school two years ago last month. I had my A certificate for typing, so got my first job, as a junior, in a solicitor's office. Mum was pleased at this, and Dad

said it was a first-class start, as it was an old-established firm. I must say that when I went for the interview, I was surprised at the windows, and the stairs up to the offices were also far from clean. There was a little waiting room, where some of the elements were missing from the gas fire, and the carpet on the floor was worn. However, Mr Heygate's office, into which I was shown for the interview, was better. The furniture was old, but it was polished, and there was a good carpet, I will say that. The glass of the bookcase was very clean.

I was to start on the Monday, so along I went. They took me to the general office, where there were two senior shorthand-typists, and a clerk, Mr Gresham, who was far from smart in appearance. You should have seen the mess!! There was no floor covering whatsoever, and so dusty everywhere. There were shelves all round the room, with old box files on them. The box files were falling to pieces, and all the old papers inside them were crumpled. The worst shock of all was the tea cups. It was my duty to make tea,

mornings and afternoons. Miss.Bewlay showed me where everything was kept. It was kept in an old orange box, and the cups were all cracked. There were not enough saucers to go round, etc. I will not go into the facilities, but they were also far from hygienic. After three days, I told Mum, and she was upset, most of all about the cracked cups. We never keep a cracked cup, but throw it out, because those cracks can harbour germs. So Mum gave me my own cup to take to the office.

Then at the end of the week, when I got my salary, Mr Heygate said, 'Well, Lorna, what are you going to do with your first pay?' I did not like him saying this, and I nearly passed a comment, but I said, 'I don't know.' He said, 'What do you do in the evenings, Lorna? Do you watch Telly?' I did take this as an insult, because we call it TV, and his remark made me out to be uneducated. I just stood, and did not answer, and he looked surprised. Next day, Saturday, I told Mum and Dad about the facilities, and we decided I should not go back to that job. Also, the desks in the general office were rickety. Dad was indignant, because Mr Heygate's concern was flourishing, and he had letters after his name.

Everyone admires our flat, because Mum keeps it spotless, and Dad keeps doing things to it. He had done it up all over, and got permission from the Council to re-modernize the kitchen. I well recall the Health Visitor, remarking to Mum, 'You could eat off your floor, Mrs Merrifield.' It is true that you could eat your lunch off Mum's floor, and any hour of the day or night you will find every corner spick and span.

Next, I was sent by the agency to a Publisher's for an interview, because of being good at English. One look was enough!! My next interview was a success, and I am still at Low's Chemical Co. It is a modern block, with a quarter of an hour rest period, morning and afternoon. Mr Marwood is very smart in appearance. He is well spoken, although he has not got a university education behind him. There is special lighting over the desks, and the typewriters are latest models.

So I am happy at Low's. But I have met other people, of an educated type, in the past year, and it has opened my eyes. It so happened that I had to go to the Doctor's house, to fetch a prescription for my young brother, Trevor, when the epidemic was on. I rang the bell, and Mrs Darby came to the door. She was small, with fair hair, but too long, and a green maternity dress. But she was very nice to me. I had to wait in their living-room, and you should have seen the state it was in! There were broken toys on the carpet, and the ash-trays were full up. There were contemporary pictures on the walls, but the furniture was not contemporary, but old-fashioned, with covers which were past standing up to another wash, I should say. To cut a long story short, Dr Darby and Mrs Darby have always been very kind to me, and they meant everything for the best. Dr Darby is also short and fair, and they have three children, a girl and a boy, and now a baby boy.

When I went that day for the prescription, Dr Darby said to me, 'You look pale, Lorna. It's the London atmosphere. Come on a picnic with us, in the car, on Saturday.' After that I went with the Darbys more and more. I like them, but I did not like the mess, and it was a surprise. But I also kept in with them for the opportunity of meeting people, and Mum and Dad were pleased that I had made nice friends. So I did not say anything about the cracked lino, and the paint-work all chipped. The children's clothes were very shabby for a Doctor, and she changed them out of their school clothes when they came home from school, into those worn-out garments. Mum always kept us spotless to go out to play, and I do not like to say it, but those Darby children frequently looked like the Leary family, which the Council evicted from our block, as they were far from houseproud.

One day, when I was there, Mavis (as I called Mrs Darby by then) put her head out of the window, and shouted to the boy, 'John, stop peeing over the cabbages at once. Pee on the lawn.' I did not know which way to look. Mum would never say a word like that from the window, and I know for a fact that Trevor would never pass water outside, not even bathing in the sea.

I went there usually at the weekends, but sometimes on week-days after supper. They had an idea to make a match for me with a chemist's assistant, whom they had taken up too. He was an orphan, and I do not say there was anything wrong with that. But he was not accustomed to those little extras that I was. He was a good-looking boy, I will say that. So I went once to a dance, and twice to the films with him. To look at, he was quite clean in appearance. But there was only hot water at the weekend at his place, and he said that a bath once a week was sufficient. Jim (as I called Dr Darby by then) said it was sufficient also, and surprised me. He did not have much money, and I do not hold that against him. But there was no hurry for me, and I could wait for a man in a better position, so that I would not miss those little extras. So he started going out with a girl from the coffee bar, and did not come to the Darbys very much then.

There were plenty of boys at the office, but I will say this for the Darbys, they had lots of friends coming and going, and they had interesting conversation, although sometimes it gave me a surprise, and I did not know where to look. And sometimes they had people who were very down and out, although there is no need to be. But most of the guests were different, so it made a comparison with the boys at the office, who were not so educated in their conversation.

Now it was near the time for Mavis to have her baby, and I was to come in at the weekend, to keep an eye on the children, while the help had her day off. Mavis did not go away to have her baby, but would have it at home, in their double bed, as they did not have twin beds, although he was a Doctor. A girl I knew, in our block, was engaged, but was let down, and even she had her baby in the labour ward. I was sure the bedroom was not hygenic for having a baby, but I did not mention it.

One day, after the baby boy came along, they took me in the car to the country, to see Jim's mother. The baby was put in a carry-cot at the back of the car. He began to cry, and without a word of a lie, Jim said to him over his shoulder, 'Oh shut your gob, you little bastard.' I did not know what to do, and Mavis was smoking a cigarette. Dad would not dream of saying such a thing to Trevor or I. When we arrived at Jim's mother's place, Jim said, 'It's a four-teenth-century cottage, Lorna.' I could well believe it. It was very cracked and old, and it made one wonder how Jim could let his old mother live in this tumble-down cottage, as he was so good to everyone else. So Mavis knocked at the door, and the old lady came. There was not much anyone could do to the inside. Mavis said, 'Isn't it charming, Lorna?' If that was a joke, it was going too far. I said to the old Mrs Darby, 'Are you going to be re-housed?' but she did not understand this, and I explained how you have to apply to the Council, and keep at them. But it was funny that the Council had not done something already, when they go round condemning. Then old Mrs Darby said, 'My dear, I shall be re-housed in the Grave.' I did not know where to look.

There was a carpet hanging on the wall, which I think was there to hide a damp spot. She had a good TV set, I will say that. But some of the walls were bare brick, and the facilities were outside, through the garden. The furniture was far from new.

One Saturday afternoon, as I happened to go to the Darbys, they were just going off to a film, and they took me too. It was the Curzon, and afterwards we went to a flat in Curzon Street. It was a very clean block, I will say that, and there were good carpets at the entrance. The couple there had contemporary furniture, and they also spoke about music. It was a nice place, but there was no Welfare Centre to the flats, where people could go for social inter-course, advice and guidance. But they were well-spoken, and I met

Willy Morley, who was an artist. Willy sat beside me, and we had a drink. He was young, dark, with a dark shirt, so one could not see right away if he was clean. Soon after this, Jim said to me, 'Willie wants to paint you, Lorna. But you'd better ask your Mum.' Mum said it was all right if he was a friend of the Darbys.

I can honestly say that Willie's place was the most unhygienic place I have seen in my life. He said I had an unusual type of beauty, which he must capture. This was when we came back to his place from the restaurant. The light was very dim, but I could see the bed had not been made, and the sheets were far from clean. He said he must paint me, but I told Mavis I did not like to go back there. 'Don't you like Willy?' she asked. I could not deny that I liked Willy, in a way. There was something about him, I will say that. Mavis said, 'I hope he hasn't been making a pass at you, Lorna.' I said he had not done so, which was almost true, because he did not attempt to go to the full extent. It was always unhygienic when I went to Willy's place, and I told him so once, but he said, 'Lorna, you are a joy.' He had a nice way, and he took me out in his car, which was a good one, but dirty inside, like his place. Jim said one day, 'He has pots of money, Lorna,' and Mavis said, 'You might make a man of him, as he is keen on you.' They always said Willy came from a good family.

But I saw that one could not do anything with him. He would not change his shirt very often, or get clothes, but he went round like a tramp, lending people money, as I have seen with my own eyes. His place was in a terrible mess, with the empty bottles, and laundry in the corner. He gave me several gifts over the period, which I took, as he would have only given them away, but he never tried to go to the full extent. He never painted my portrait, as he was painting fruit on a table all that time, and they said his pictures were marvellous, and thought Willy and I were getting married.

One night, when I went home, I was upset as usual, after Willy's place. Mum and Dad had gone to bed, and I looked round our kitchen which is done in primrose and white. Then I went into the living-room, where Dad has done one wall in a patterned paper, deep rose and white, and the other walls pale rose, with white woodwork. The suite is new, and Mum keeps everything beautiful. So it came to me, all of a sudden, what a fool I was, going with Willy. I agree to equality, but as to me marrying Willy, as I said to Mavis, when I recall his place, and the good carpet gone greasy, not to mention the paint oozing out of the tubes, I think it would break my heart to sink so low.

MURIEL SPARK *The Go-Away Bird and Other Stories*

The Big Decision

She put down the receiver and picked up her book again. Of course, she didn't read it, and a few moments later it was slung across the room.

'I hate you!' she roared at the telephone. It didn't answer. 'I hate you, I hate you, with your lies and your girls and your casualness!'

She went to the other wall and picked up the book.

'I'll show you,' she said. 'This time it's for real,' she thought. All the time it was just lies and teasing. Well, she had had enough. There was just so much a girl could take.

She lifted the receiver, then dropped it again. No, not like that. It was too ordinary. He would never remember that, and this had to be special. She closed the book carefully and put it down. Half an hour. For a start she could look beautiful. That wasn't difficult.

Almost a year, now. She hated him.

Testing the bath water, she laughed aloud at him – just so the girl next door would think she was mad. They all thought that. They had all very probably been laughing at her all along. Even him. She laughed again, and realized the water was too hot.

'Damn the whole lot of you!' she shouted. Grabbing handfuls of clothes she marched back into the bathroom.

She was a fool; that was certain. Correction. She *had* been a fool. But not now. The water was too cold, now, but it didn't matter.

Oh, how she hated him. How she was going to hurt him. Just the same way he had hurt her. Kid him on a bit, then the cold shoulder, do-I-know-you? routine. Only for always and always, now. He would get hurt this time.

He would guess at once that something was wrong by her slightly bored look. She practised her slightly-bored look in the mirror. It looked as though she were trying hard not to cry or something. Or she could be terribly distracted about something (somebody?) That was it. As though he were rather in the way. If only she could stop that damn shivering. It was the water.

She dressed hurriedly. Quarter of an hour. What if he were early just to spite her? That would be just like him. Well, she would be ready.

All those lies. Oh, it made her mad to think of how long she had put up with it. Madness! From now on he would be the fool. That lie about last night for a start. It was obvious to anyone that it was a lie. And his ringing up and being sorry didn't change anything. And why in heaven's name did he always have to keep on about his girl-friends? 'What's wrong in having friends, then?' All the time. Remarks like that. Anyway, it was the last remark of that type he had made as far as she was concerned.

'If only I wasn't such a kind-hearted bitch,' she thought, as she frowned at her eye-shadow in the mirror. Then, because she liked the sound of it, she shouted, 'Bitch! Kind-hearted bitch!' at the slightly-bored looking face in front of her. 'I just hope she heard that next door,' she thought.

Five minutes. She draped herself casually over the sofa, adjusting her expression. He was bound to be early. How she hated him! She would say: 'Well, I've had enough and there it is.' Semi-dramatic type of scene, or the down-to-earth, crude: 'Right, mate, you've had your chips with this number.' He wouldn't appreciate that. He'd probably laugh, not seeing the subtlety behind what she had said.

He would cry, or something, just to get round her. Then she would laugh drily. She practised a few dry laughs. They sounded nervous. There was a nasty taste in her mouth all of a sudden. She rushed in the bathroom and brushed her teeth. What if he came while she was brushing them? Let him wait. She rushed back.

'Damn, damn, damn!' she shouted, searching for a lip-stick. 'Oh, damn!'

She draped herself again. He was five minutes late already. She had known that would happen. Right up to the last he had to keep her in suspense. Only he didn't know it was the last. That was the big laugh. He would be there in a minute. All smiles and kisses and apologies. Let him keep his rotten kisses, or rather, give them to one of his other girl-friends, from now on. It sounded so final. Well, she was glad. And she was glad he was a quarter of an hour late, too. It only made her hate him the more. It wasn't exactly a quarter, because that clock was fast, and she wasn't sure just how much. But he was late. Oh, yes. He was late enough.

All those beautiful kisses, and those beautiful, beautiful words. It made her sick. He was going to look so small. So lost. How she was going to love it! Every minute of picking him to pieces and saying just what she thought for a change. Just as well he hadn't asked her to marry him, or anything. She would say it very softly and as if she was uninvolved. As if it were two completely different people she was talking about. That was it. Oh, she was going to laugh. If only she could stop shivering. It was that damned central heating.

Twenty-five minutes. Perhaps he wasn't coming at all. Of course he was, and God, wasn't she going to clean him when he did.

It wasn't all bad times, though, and he had made her want to be beautiful. Just because she was a big fool. She was going to enjoy this.

It was very dark beyond the window, now. It was raining, too. She hadn't noticed that. He was bound to give that as tonight's excuse. If he bothered.

Well, she wasn't bothering any more, anyway. She went into the kitchen to make some coffee, and frisk herself for blotches in the mirror.

It hadn't been so bad in the summer, but it was different, now. And what was more it was windy out there, and howling, and she wanted to cry because she hated him so much. All the stupid things he said, and the way he grinned, and danced and kissed and spoke. The way he hurt her again and again, and pretended all the time he didn't know he had. She was going to hurt him, now. Oh, how he was going to get hurt!

The bell rang suddenly, and she stood motionless, shivering. She opened the door.

It was him. Hands behind his back, and grinning like a little boy. Water pouring off him everywhere. What a mess he looked! The hands moved swiftly forwards, and the flowers tumbled out of them. So many, many flowers. So many beautiful, lovely flowers. And what with the wetness and the laughing and the excuse there in his beautiful hands, the tears just had to come, and he pressed her to him so she was a part of the wetness and the smell of rain.

'Darling . . . darling.' Oh, she hated him. Soon she would tear out his hair, and trample on him. But now she must kiss him, and now they must both cry, and both laugh, and tremble against each other in the coldness.

Oh, the hatred, and it was all a wonderful, wonderful part of loving him!

LESLEY ANNE HAYES *aged 14*

Flame on the Frontier

On Sunday morning, wearing white man's sober clothing, a Sioux chief named Little Crow attended the church service at the Lower Agency and afterwards shook hands with the preacher. On Sunday afternoon, Little Crow's painted and feathered Santee Sioux swooped down on the settlers in bloody massacre. There was no warning. . . .

Hannah Harris spoke sharply to her older daughter, Mary Amanda. 'I've told you twice to get more butter from the spring. Now step! The men want to eat.'

The men – Oscar Harris and his two sons, sixteen and eighteen – sat in stolid patience on a bench in front of the cabin, waiting to be called to the table.

Mary Amanda put down the book she had borrowed from a distant neighbour and went unwillingly out of the cabin. She liked to read and was proud that she knew how, but she never had another book in her hands as long as she lived. Mary Amanda Harris was, on that day in August in 1862, just barely thirteen years old.

Her little sister Sarah tagged along down to the spring for lack of anything better to do. She was healthily hungry, and the smell of frying chicken had made her fidget until her mother had warned, 'Am I going to have to switch you?'

The two girls wrangled as they trotted down the accustomed path.

'Now what'd you come tagging for?' demanded Mary Amanda. She wanted to stay, undisturbed, in the world of the book she had been reading.

Sarah said, 'I guess I got a right to walk here as good as you.'

She shivered, not because of any premonition but simply because the air was cool in the brush by the spring. She glanced across the narrow creek and saw a paint-striped face. Before she could finish her scream, the Indian had leaped the creek and smothered her mouth.

At the cabin they heard that single, throat-tearing scream instantly muffled. They knew what had to be done; they had planned it, because this day might come to any frontier farm.

Hannah Harris scooped up the baby boy, Willie, and hesitated only to cry out, 'The girls?'

The father, already inside the cabin, handed one rifle to his eldest son as he took the other for himself. To Jim, who was sixteen, he barked, 'The axe, boy.'

Hannah knew what she had to do – run and hide – but that part of the plan had included the little girls, too. She was to take the four younger children, including the dull boy, Johnny. She was too sick with the meaning of that brief scream to be able to change the plan and go without the girls.

But Oscar roared, 'Run for the rushes! You crazy?' and broke her paralysis. With the baby under one arm she began to run down the hill to a place by the river where the rushes grew high.

The only reason Hannah was able to get to the rushes with her two youngest boys was that the men, Oscar and Jim and Zeke, delayed the Indians for a few minutes. The white men might have barricaded themselves in the cabin and stood off the attackers for a longer period, but the approaching Indians would have seen that frantic scuttling into the rushes.

Oscar and Jim and Zeke did not defend. They attacked. With the father going first, they ran towards the spring and met the Indians in the brush. Fighting there, they bought a little time for the three to hide down by the river, and they paid for it with their lives.

Hannah, the mother, chose another way of buying time. She heard the invaders chopping at whatever they found in the cabin. She heard their howls as they found clothing and kettles and food. She stayed in the rushes as long as she dared, but when she smelled the smoke of the cabin burning, she knew the Indians would be ranging out to see what else might be found.

Then she thrust the baby into Johnny's arms, and said fiercely. 'You take care of him and don't you let him go until they kill you.'

She did not give him any instructions about how to get to a place of safety. There might be no such place.

She kissed Johnny on the forehead and she kissed the baby twice, because he was so helpless and because he was, blessedly, not crying.

She crawled to the left, far to the left of the children, so that she would not be seen coming directly from their hiding place. Then she came dripping up out of the rushes and went shrieking up the hill straight towards the Indians.

When they started down to meet her, she hesitated and turned. She ran, still screaming, towards the river, as if she were so crazed she did not know what she was doing. But she knew. She knew very well. She did exactly what a meadowlark will do if its nest in the grass is menaced – she came into the open, crying and frantic, and lured the pursuit away from her young.

But the meadowlark acts by instinct, not by plan. Hannah Harris had to fight down her instinct, which was to try to save her own life.

As the harsh hands seized her, she threw her arm across her eyes so as not to see death. . . .

Of the two girls down at the spring, only Sarah screamed. Mary Amanda did not have time. A club, swung easily by a strong arm, cracked against her head.

Sarah Harris heard the brief battle and knew her father's voice, but she did not have to see the bodies, a few yards away on the path, through the brush. One of the Indians held her without difficulty. She was a thin little girl, nine years old.

Mary Amanda was unconscious and would have drowned except that her guard pulled her out of the creek and laid her, face down, on the gravel bank.

The girls never saw their cabin again. Their captors tied their hands behind them and headed back the way they had come to rejoin the war party. The girls were too frightened to cry or speak. They stumbled through the brush.

Mary Amanda fell too many times. Finally she gave up and lay still, waiting to die, sobbing quietly. Her guard grunted and lifted his club.

Sarah flew at him shrieking. Her hands were tied, but her feet were free and she could still run.

'Don't you hurt my sister!' she scolded. 'Don't you do it, I say!' She bowed her head and bunted him.

The Indian, who had never had anything to do with white people except at a distance, or in furious flurries of raiding, was astonished by her courage, and impressed. All he knew of white girls was that they ran away, screaming, and then were caught. This one had the desperate, savage fury of his own women. She chattered as angrily as a bluejay. (Bluejay was the name he gave her, the name everyone called her, in the years she lived and grew up among the Sioux.)

She had knocked the wind out of him, but he was amused. He jerked the older girl, Mary Amanda, to her feet.

The mother, Hannah, was taken along by the same route, about a mile behind them, but she did not know they were still alive. One of them she saw again six years later. The other girl she never saw again.

For hours she went stumbling, praying, 'Lord in thy mercy, make them kill me fast!'

When they did not, she let hope flicker, and when they camped that night, she began to ask timidly, 'God, could you help me get away?'

She had no food that night, and no water. An Indian had tied her securely.

The following day her captors caught up with a larger party, carrying much loot and driving three other white women. They were younger than Hannah. That was what saved her.

When she was an old woman, she told the tale grimly: 'I prayed to the Lord to let me go, and He turned the Indians' backs on me and I went into the woods, and that was how I got away.'

She did not tell how she would still hear the piercing shrieks of the other white women, even when she was far enough into the woods so that she dared to run.

She blundered through the woods, hiding at every sound, praying to find a trail, but terrified when she came to one, for fear there might be Indians around the next bend. After she reached the trail and began to follow it, she had a companion, a shaggy yellow dog.

For food during two days she had berries. Then she came upon the dog eating a grouse he had killed, and she stooped, but he growled.

'Nice doggie,' she crooned. 'Nice old Sheppy.'

She abased herself with such praise until – probably because he had caught other game and was not hungry – he let her take the tooth-torn, dirt-smeared remnants. She picked off the feathers with fumbling fingers, washed the raw meat in the creek and ate it as she walked.

She smelled wood smoke the next morning and crawled through brush until she could see a clearing. She saw white people there in front of a cabin, and much bustling. She heard children crying and the authoritative voices of women. She stood up then and ran, screaming, towards the cabin, with the dog jumping and barking beside her.

One of the hysterical women there seized a rifle and fired a shot at Hannah before a man shouted. 'She's white!' and ran out to meet her.

There were sixteen persons in the cramped cabin or near it – refugees from other farms. Hannah Harris kept demanding, while she wolfed down food. 'Ain't anybody seen two little girls? Ain't anybody seen a boy and a baby?'

Nobody had seen them.

The draggled-skirted women in the crowded cabin kept busy with their children, but Hannah Harris had no children any more – she who had had four sons and two daughters. She dodged among the refugees, beseeching, 'Can't I help with something? Ain't there anything I can do?'

A busy old woman said with sharp sympathy, 'Miz Harris, you go lay down some place. Git some sleep. All you been through '

Hannah Harris understood that there was no room for her there. She stumbled outside and lay down in a grassy place in the shade. She slept, no longer hearing the squalling of babies and the wrangling of the women.

Hannah awoke to the crying of voices she knew and ran around to the front of the cabin. She saw two men carrying a stretcher made of two shirts buttoned around poles. A bundle sagged on the stretcher, and a woman was trying to lift it, but it cried with two voices.

Johnny lay there, clutching the baby, and both of them were screaming.

Kneeling, she saw blood on Johnny's feet and thought with horror. 'Did the Injuns do that?' Then she remembered, 'No, he was barefoot when we ran.'

He would not release the baby, even for her. He was gaunt, his ribs showed under his tattered shirt. His eyes were partly open, and his lips were drawn back from his teeth. He was only half conscious, but he still had strength enough to clutch his baby brother, though the baby screamed with hunger and fear.

Hannah said in a strong voice, 'Johnny, you can let go now. You can let Willie go. Johnny, this is your mother talking.'

With a moan, he let his arms go slack.

For the rest of his life, and he lived another fifty years, he suffered from nightmares, and often awoke screaming.

With two of her children there Hannah Harris was the equal of any woman. She pushed among the others to get to the food, to find cloth for Johnny's wounded feet. She wrangled with them, defending sleeping space for her children.

For a few months she made a home for her boys by keeping house for a widower named Lincoln Bartlett, whose two daughters had been killed at a neighbour's cabin. Then she married him.

The baby, Willie, did not live to grow up, in spite of the sacrifices that had been made for him. He died of diphtheria. While Link Bartlett dug a little grave, Hannah sat, stern but dry-eyed, on a slab bench, cradling the still body in her arms.

The dull boy, Johnny, burst out hoarsely, 'It wasn't no use after all, was it?' and his mother understood.

She told him strongly, 'Oh, yes, it was! It was worth while, all you did. He's dead now, but he died in my arms, with a roof over him. I'll know where he's buried. It ain't as if the Indians had butchered him some place that I'd never know.'

She carried the body across the room and laid it tenderly in the box that had been Willie's bed and would be his coffin. She turned to her other son and said, 'Johnny, come sit on my lap.'

He was a big boy, twelve years old, and he was puzzled by this invitation, as he was puzzled about so many things. Awkwardly he sat on her knees, and awkwardly he permitted her to cuddle his head against her shoulder.

'How long since your mother kissed you? she asked, and he mumbled back, 'Don't know.'

She kissed his forehead. 'You're my big boy. You're my Johnny.'

He lay in her arms for a while, tense and puzzled. After a while, not knowing why it was necessary to cry, he began to sob, and she rocked him back and forth. She had no tears left.

Johnny said something then that he had thought over many times, often enough to be sure about it. 'It was him that mattered most, I guess.'

Hannah looked down at him, shocked.

'He was my child and I loved him,' she said. 'It was him I worried about. . . . But it was you I trusted.'

The boy blinked and scowled. His mother bowed her head.

'I never said so. I thought you knowed that. When I give him to you that day, Johnny boy, I put more trust in you than I did in the Lord God.'

That was a thing he always remembered – the time his mother made him understand that for a while he had been more important than God.

The Harris sisters were sold twice, the second time to a Sioux warrior named Runs Buffalo, whose people ranged far to the westward.

Bluejay never had to face defeat among the Indians. The little girl who had earned her name by scolding angrily had the privileges of a baby girl. She was fed and cared for like the Indian children, and she had more freedom and less scolding than she had had in the cabin that was burned. Like the other little girls, she was freer than the boys. Her responsibility would not begin for three or four years. When the time came, she would be taught to do the slow, patient work of the women, in preparation for being a useful wife. But while she was little, she could play.

While the boys learned to shoot straight and follow tracks, while they tested and increased their endurance and strength, the little girls played and laughed in the sun. Bluejay did not even have a baby to look after, because she was the youngest child in the lodge of Runs Buffalo. She was the petted one, the darling, and the only punishment she knew was what she deserved for profaning holy objects. Once at home she had been switched by her father for putting a dish on the great family Bible. In the Indian village, she learned to avoid touching medicine bundles or sacred shields and to keep silent in the presence of men who understood religious mysteries.

Mary Amanda, stooped over a raw buffalo hide, scraping it hour after hour with tools of iron and bone, because that was the women's work and she was almost a woman, heard familiar shrill arguments among the younger girls, the same arguments that had sounded in the white settlement, and in the same language: 'You're it!' . . . 'I am not!'

That much the little Indian girls learned of English. Sarah learned Sioux so fast that she no longer needed English and would have stopped speaking it except that her older sister insisted.

Mary Amanda learned humility through blows. To her, everything about the Indians was contemptible. She learned their language simply to keep from being cuffed by the older women, who were less shocked at her ignorance of their skills than at her unwillingness to learn the work that was a woman's privilege to perform. She sickened at the business of softening hides with a mixture of clay and buffalo manure. If she had been more docile, she might have been an honoured daughter in the household. Instead, she was a sullen slave. Mary Amanda remembered what Sarah often forgot: that she was white. Mary Amanda never stopped hoping that they would be rescued. The name the Indians gave her was The Foreigner.

When she tried to take Sarah aside to talk English, the old woman of the household scolded.

Mary Amanda spoke humbly in Sioux. 'Bluejay forgets to talk like our own people. I want her to know how to talk.'

The old woman growled, 'You are Indians,' and Mary Amanda answered, 'It is good for Indians to be able to talk to white people.'

The argument was sound. A woman interpreter would never be permitted in the councils of chiefs and captains, but who could tell when the skill might be useful? The girls were allowed to talk together, but Sarah preferred Sioux.

When The Foreigner was sixteen years old she had four suitors. She knew what a young man meant by sending a gift of meat to the lodge and later standing out in front, blanket-wrapped and silent.

When the young man came, Mary Amanda pretended not to notice, and the old woman pretended with her, but there was chuckling in the lodge as everyone waited to see whether The Foreigner would go out, perhaps to bring in water from the creek.

Her little sister teased her. 'Go on out. All you have to do is let him put his blanket around you and talk. Go on. Other girls do.'

'Indian girls do,' Mary Amanda answered sadly. 'That ain't the way boys do their courting back home.'

The tall young men were patient. Sometimes as many as three at once stood out there through twilight into darkness, silent and waiting. They were eligible, respected young men, skilled in hunting and taking horses, proved in courage, schooled in the mysteries of protective charms and chanted prayer. All of them had counted coup in battle.

hit an enemy

Mary Amanda felt herself drawn towards the lodge opening. It would be so easy to go out!

She asked Sarah humbly, 'Do you think it's right, the way they buy their wives? Of course, the girl's folks give presents to pay back.'

Sarah shrugged. 'What other way is there? . . . If it was me, I'd go out fast enough. Just wait till I'm older!' She reminded her sister of something it was pleasanter to forget. 'They don't have to wait for you to make up your mind. They could sell you to an old man for a third wife.'

When Mary Amanda was seventeen, a man of forty, who had an ageing wife, looked at her with favour, and she made her choice. On a sweet summer evening she arose from her place in the tepee and, without a word to anyone, stooped and passed through the lodge opening. She was trembling as she walked past Hawk and Grass Runner and eluded their reaching hands. She stopped before a young man named Snow Mountain.

He was as startled as the family back in the tepee. Courting The Foreigner had become almost a tradition with the young men, because she seemed unattainable and competition ruled their lives. He wrapped his blanket around her and felt her heart beating wildly.

He did not tell her she was pretty. He told her that he was brave and cunning. He told her he was a skilled hunter, his lodge never lacked for meat. He had many horses, most of them stolen from the Crows in quick, desperate raids.

Mary Amanda said, 'You give horses to buy what you want. Will Runs Buffalo gives presents to you in return?'

That was terribly important to her. The exchange of gifts was in itself the ceremony. If she went to him with no dowry, she went without honour.

'I cannot ask about that,' he said. 'My mother's brother will ask.'

But Runs Buffalo refused.

'I will sell the white woman for horses,' he announced. 'She belongs to me. I paid for her.'

Mary Amanda went without ceremony, on a day in autumn, to the new lodge of Snow Mountain. She went without pride, without dowry. The lodge was new and fine, she had the tools and kettles she needed, and enough robes to keep the household warm. But all the household things were from his people, not hers. When she cried, he comforted her.

For her there was no long honeymoon of lazy bliss. Her conscience made her keep working to pay Snow Mountain for the gifts no one had given him. But she was no longer a slave, she was queen in her own household. An old woman, a relative of his mother, lived with them to do heavy work. Snow Mountain's youngest brother lived with him, helping to hunt and butcher and learning the skills a man needed to know.

Mary Amanda was a contented bride – except when she remembered that she had not been born an Indian. And there was always in her mind the knowledge that many warriors had two wives, and that often the two wives were sisters.

'You work too hard,' Snow Mountain told her. 'Your little sister does not work hard enough.'

'She is young,' The Foreigner reminded him, feeling that she should apologize for Bluejay's shortcomings.

Snow Mountain said, 'When she is older, maybe she will come here.'

Afterwards she knew he meant that in kindness. But thinking of Sarah as her rival in the tepee, as her sister-wife, froze Mary Amanda's heart. She answered only, 'Bluejay is young.'

Sarah Harris, known as Bluejay, already had two suitors when she was only fourteen. One of them was only two or three years older than she was, and not suitable for a husband; he had few war honours and was not very much respected by anyone except his own parents. The other was a grown man, a young warrior named Horse Ears, very suitable and, in fact, better than the flighty girl had any right to expect.

When Sarah visited in her sister's lodge, she boasted of the two young men.

Mary Amanda cried out, 'Oh, no! You're too young to take a man. You could wait two years yet, maybe three. Sarah, some day you will go back home.'

Two years after the massacre, the first rumour that the Harris girls were alive reached the settlement, but it was nothing their mother could put much faith in. The rumour came in a roundabout way, to Link Bartlett, Hannah's second husband, from a soldier at the fort, who had it from another soldier, who had it from a white trader, who heard it from a Cheyenne. And all they heard was that two white sisters were with a Sioux village far to the westward. Rumours like that drifted in constantly. Two hundred women had been missing after that raid.

Two more years passed before they could be fairly sure that there were really two white sisters out there and that they were probably the Harrises.

After still another year, the major who commanded the army post nearest the settlement was himself convinced, and negotiations began for their ransom.

Link Bartlett raised every cent he could – he sold some of his best land – to buy the gifts for that ransom.

In the sixth year of the captivity, a cavalry detachment was ordered out on a delicate diplomatic mission – to find and buy the girls back, if possible.

Link Bartlett had his own horse saddled and was ready to leave the cabin, to go with the soldiers, when Hannah cried harshly, 'Link, don't you go! Don't go away and leave me and the kids!'

The children were dull Johnny and a two-year-old boy, named Lincoln, after his father, the last child Hannah ever had.

Link tried to calm her. 'Now, Hannah, you know we planned I should go along to see they got back all right – if we can find 'em at all.'

'I ain't letting you go,' she said, 'If them soldiers can't make out without you, they're a poor lot.' Then she jarred him to his heels. She said, almost gently, 'Link, if I was to lose you, I'd die.'

That was the only time she ever hinted that she loved him. He never asked for any more assurance. He stayed at home because she wanted him there.

Mary Amanda's son was half a year old when the girls first learned there was hope of their being ransomed.

The camp crier, walking among the lodges, wailed out the day's news so that everyone in the village would know what was planned: 'Women, stay in the camp. Keep your children close to you where they will be safe. There is danger. Some white soldiers are camped on the other side of the hills. Three men will go out and talk to them. The three men are Runs Buffalo, Big Moon and Snow Mountain.'

Mary Amanda did not dare ask Snow Mountain anything. She watched him ride out with the other men, and then she sat on the ground in front of his tepee, nursing her baby. Bluejay came to the lodge and the two girls sat together in silence as the hours passed.

The men from the Sioux camp did not come back until three days later. When Snow Mountain was ready to talk, he remarked, 'The white soldiers came to find out about two white girls. They will bring presents to pay if the white girls want to go back.'

Mary Amanda answered, 'O-o-oh,' in a sigh like a frail breeze in prairie grass.

There was no emotion in his dark, stern face. He looked at her for a long moment, and at the baby. Then he turned away without explanation. She called after him, but he did not answer. She felt the dark eyes staring, heard the low voices. She was a stranger again, as she had not been for a long time.

Nothing definite had been decided at the parley with the white soldiers, the girls learned. The soldiers would come back sometime, bringing presents for ransom, and if the presents were fine enough, there would be talk and perhaps a bargain. Mary Amanda felt suddenly the need to prepare Sarah for life in the settlement. She told her everything she could remember that might be useful.

'You'll cook over a fire in a fireplace,' she said, 'and sew with thread, and you'll have to learn to knit.'

Bluejay whimpered, 'I wish you could come, too.'

'He wouldn't let me go, of course,' Mary Amanda answered complacently. 'He wouldn't let me take the baby, and I wouldn't leave without *him*. You tell them I got a good man. Be sure to tell them that.'

At night, remembering the lost heaven of the burned cabin, remembering the life that was far away and long ago, she cried a little. But she did not even consider begging Snow Mountain to let her go. She had offended him, but when he stopped brooding they would talk again. He had not said anything to her since he had tested her by telling her the ransom had been offered.

He did not even tell her that he was going away. He gave orders to the old woman in the lodge and discussed plans with his younger brother, but he ignored his wife. Five men were going out to take horses from the Crows, he said. Mary Amanda shivered.

Before he rode away with his war party, he spent some time playing with the baby, bouncing the child on his knee, laughing when the baby laughed. But he said nothing to Mary Amanda, and the whole village knew that he was angry and that she deserved his anger.

Her hands and feet were cold as she watched him go, and her

heart was gnawed by the fear that was part of every Indian woman's life: 'Maybe he will never come back.'

Not until the white soldiers had come back to parley again did she understand how cruelly she had hurt him.

She dreamed of home while they waited for news of the parley, and she tried to make Bluejay dream of it.

'You'll have to do some things different there, but Ma will remind you. I'll bet Ma will cry like everything when she sees you coming.' Mary Amanda's eyes flooded with tears, seeing that meeting. 'I don't remember she ever did cry,' she added thoughtfully, 'but I guess she must have sometimes. . . . Ma must have got out of it all right. Who else would be sending the ransom? Oh, well, sometime I'll find out all about it from Snow Mountain. . . . I wonder if she got Johnny and Willie away from the cabin safe. Tell her I talked about her lots. Be sure to tell Ma that, Sarah. Tell her how cute my baby is.'

Bluejay, unnaturally silent, dreamed with her, wide-eyed, of the reunion, the half-forgotten heaven of the settlement.

'Tell her about Snow Mountain,' Mary Amanda reminded her sister. 'Be sure to do that. How he's a good hunter, so we have everything we want, and more. And everybody respects him. Tell her he's good to me and the baby. . . . But, Sarah, don't ever say he steals horses. They wouldn't understand, back home. . . . And don't ever let on a word about scalps. If they say anything about scalps, you say our people here don't do that.'

'They do, though,' Sarah reminded her flatly. 'It takes a brave man to stop and take a scalp off when somebody's trying to kill him.'

Looking at her, Mary Amanda realized that Sarah didn't even think taking scalps was bad, so long as your own people did it and didn't have it done to them.

'You're going to have to forget some things,' she warned with a sigh.

While the parley was still on, Big Moon, the medicine priest, came to the lodge where The Foreigner bent over her endless work. He was carrying something wrapped in buckskin.

"Tell them the names of the people in your lodge before you came to the Sioux,' he said shortly as he put down the buckskin bundle. 'They are not sure you are the women they want.'

In the bundle were sheets of paper and a black crayon.

Sarah came running. She sat fascinated as Mary Amanda wrote carefully on the paper: 'Popa, Moma, Zeke, Jim, Johny, Wily.'

Mary Amanda was breathless when she finished. She squeezed Sarah's arm. 'Just think, you're going to go home!'

Sarah nodded, not speaking. Sarah was getting scared.

The following day, the ransom was paid and brought into camp. Then The Foreigner learned how much she had offended Snow Mountain.

Big Moon brought fine gifts to the lodge, and piled them inside – a gun, powder and percussion caps and bullets, bolts of cloth, mirrors and beads and tools and a copper kettle.

'The Foreigner can go now,' he said.

Mary Amanda stared. 'I cannot go back to the white people. I am Snow Mountain's woman. This is his baby.'

'The gifts pay also for the baby,' Big Moon growled. 'Snow Mountain will have another wife, more sons. He does not need The Foreigner. He has sold her to the white man.'

Mary Amanda turned pale. 'I will not go with the white men,' she said angrily. 'When Snow Mountain comes back, he will see how much The Foreigner's people cared for her. They have sent these gifts as her dowry.'

Big Moon scowled. 'Snow Mountain may not come back. He had a dream, and the dream was bad. His heart is sick, and he does not want to come back.'

As a widow in the Sioux camp, her situation would be serious. She could not go back to her parents' home, for she had no parents. But neither could she leave the camp now to go back to the settlement and never know whether Snow Mountain was alive or dead. Sarah stood staring at her in horror.

'I will wait for him,' Mary Amanda said, choking. 'Will Big Moon pray and make medicine for him?'

The fierce old man stared at her, scowling. He knew courage when he saw it, and he admired one who dared to gamble for high stakes.

'All these gifts will belong to Big Moon,' she promised, 'if Snow Mountain comes back.'

The medicine priest nodded and turned away. 'Bluejay must come with me,' he said briefly. 'I will take her to the white soldiers and tell them The Foreigner does not want to come.'

She watched Sarah walk away between the lodges after the medicine priest. She waved good-bye, and then went into the lodge. The old woman said, 'Snow Mountain has a good wife. . . .'

Ten days passed before the war party came back. Mary Amanda waited, hardly breathing, as they brought Snow Mountain into camp tied on a travois, a pony drag.

platform or net dragged along the ground

Big Moon said, 'His shadow is gone out of his body. I do not know whether it will come back to stay.'

'I think it will come back to stay,' said The Foreigner, 'because I have prayed and made a sacrifice.'

At the sound of her voice, Snow Mountain opened his eyes. He lay quiet in his pain, staring up at her, not believing. She saw tears on his dark cheeks.

Her name was always The Foreigner, but for the rest of her life she was a woman of the Santee Sioux.

Sarah Harris, who had been called Bluejay, was hard to tame, they said in the settlement. Her mother fretted over her heathen ways. The girl could not even make bread!

'I can tan hides,' Sarah claimed angrily. 'I can butcher a buffalo and make pemmican. I can pitch a tepee and pack it on a horse to move.'

preparation of dried, pounded buffalo meat and melted fat

But those skills were not valued in a white woman, and Sarah found the settlement not quite heaven. She missed the constant talk and laughter of the close-pitched tepees. She had to learn a whole new system of polite behaviour. There was dickering and trading and bargaining, instead of a proud exchange of fine gifts. A neighbour boy slouching on a bench outside the cabin, talking to her stepfather while he got up courage to ask whether Sarah was at home, was less flattering as a suitor than a young warrior, painted and feathered, showing off on a spotted horse. Sometimes Sarah felt that she had left heaven behind her.

But she never went back to it. When she was seventeen, she married the blacksmith, Herman Schwartz, and their first baby was born six months later.

Sarah's child was six and her second child was three when the Indian man appeared at the door of her cabin and stood silently peering in.

'Git out of here!' she cried, seizing the broom.

He answered in the Sioux tongue, 'Bluejay has forgotten.'

She gave Horse Ears a shrill welcome in his own language and the three-year-old started to cry. She lifted a hand for an accustomed slap but let it fall. Indian mothers did not slap their children.

But she was not Indian any more, she recollected. She welcomed Horse Ears in as a white woman does an invited guest. In her Sunday-company voice she chatted politely. It was her privilege because she was a white woman. No need any more for the meek silence of the Indian woman.

She brought out bread and butter and ate with him. That was her privilege, too.

'My sister?' she asked.

He had not seen The Foreigner for a long time. He had left that village.

'Does Bluejay's man make much meat?' Horse Ears asked. 'Is he a man with many honours in war?'

She laughed shrilly. 'He makes much meat. He has counted coup many times. We are rich.'

'I came to find out those things,' he answered. 'In my lodge there is only one woman.'

She understood, and her heart leaped with the flattery. He had travelled far, and in some danger, to find out that all was well with her. If it was not, there was refuge in his tepee. And not only now, she realized, but any time, forever.

A shadow fell across the threshold; a hoarse voice filled the room. 'What's that bloody Injun doing here?' roared Sarah's husband. 'Are you all right?'

'Sure, we're all right,' she answered. 'I don't know who he is. He was hungry.'

His eyes narrowed with anger. 'Is he one of them you used to know?'

Her body tensed with fear. 'I don't know him, I told you!'

Her husband spoke to the Indian in halting Sioux, but Horse Ears was wise. He did not answer.

'Git out!' the blacksmith ordered, and the Indian obeyed without a word.

As Sarah watched him go down the path, without turning, she wished fervently that she could tell him good-bye, could thank him for coming. But she could not betray him by speaking.

Herman Schwartz strode towards her in silent, awesome, blazing fury. She did not cringe; she braced her body against the table. He gave her a blow across the face that rocked her and blinded her.

cooking pot   She picked up the heavy iron skillet.

'Don't you ever do that again or I'll kill you,' she warned.

He glared at her with fierce pride, knowing that she meant what she said.

'I don't reckon I'll have to do it again,' he said complacently. 'If I ever set eyes on that savage again, I'll kill him. You know that, don't you, you damn squaw?'

She shrugged. 'Talk's cheap.'

As she went down to the spring for a bucket of water, she was singing.

Her girlhood was gone, and her freedom was far behind her. She had two crying children and was pregnant again. But two men loved her, and both of them had just proved it.

Forty years later, her third child was elected to the state legislature, and she went, a frightened, white-haired widow, to see him there. She was proud, but never so proud as she had been on a summer day three months before he was born.

DOROTHY M. JOHNSON

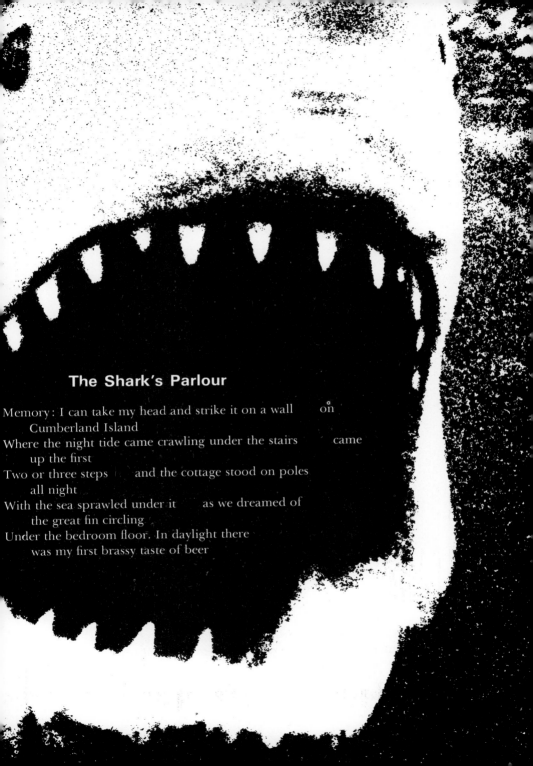

The Shark's Parlour

Memory: I can take my head and strike it on a wall   on
    Cumberland Island
Where the night tide came crawling under the stairs   came
    up the first
Two or three steps   and the cottage stood on poles
    all night
With the sea sprawled under it   as we dreamed of
    the great fin circling
Under the bedroom floor. In daylight there
    was my first brassy taste of beer

And Payton Ford and I came back from the Glynn County
    slaughterhouse

mooring rope With a bucket of entrails and blood. We tied one end of a hawser
tall and frail To a spindling porch pillar and rowed straight out of the house

Three hundred yards into the vast front yard of windless blue
    water

The rope outslithering its coil   the two gallon jug stoppered
    and sealed

With wax   and a ten-foot chain leader   a drop-forged shark
    hook nestling.

We cast our blood on the waters   the land blood easily passing

For sea blood   and we sat in it for a moment with the stain
    spreading

Out from the boat   sat in a new radiance   in the pond of
    blood in the sea

Waiting for fins   waiting to spill our guts also in the glowing
    water.

We dumped the bucket, and baited the hook with a run-over
    collie pup. The jug

Bobbed, trying to shake off the sun as a dog would shake off the
    sea.

We rowed to the house   feeling the same water lift the boat a
    new way,

All the time seeing where we lived rise and dip with the oars.

We tied up and sat down in rocking chairs, one eye or the other
    responding

To the blue-eye wink of the jug. Payton got us a beer and we sat

All morning sat there with blood on our minds   the red mark
    out

In the harbour slowly failing us   then   the house groaned
    the rope

Sprang out of the water   splinters flew   we leapt from our
    chairs

And grabbed the rope   hauled   did nothing   the house
    coming subtly

Apart   all around us   underfoot   boards beginning to
    sparkle like sand.

With the glinting of the bright hidden parts of ten-year-old nails

Pulling out the tarred poles we slept propped-up on   leaning
    to sea

As in land wind   crabs scuttling from under the floor   as we
    took turns about

Two more porch pillars   and looked out and saw
      something   a fish flash

churning An almighty fin in trouble   a moiling of secret forces   a
      false start
Of water   a round wave growing: in the whole of Cumberland
      Sound the one ripple.
Payton took off without a word   I could not hold him either
But clung to the rope anyway: it was the whole house bending
Its nails that held whatever it was   coming in a little and like a
      fool
I took up the slack on my wrist. The rope drew gently   jerked
      I lifted
Clean off the porch and hit the water   the same water it was in
I felt in a blue blazing terror at the bottom of the stairs and
      scrambled
Back up looking desperately into the human house as deeply as I
      could
Stopping my gaze before it went out the wire screen of the back
      door

climbing palm Stopped it on the thistled rattan   the rugs I lay on and read
On mother's sewing basket with next winter's socks spilling from
      it
The flimsy vacation furniture   a bucktoothed picture of myself.
Payton came back with three men from a filling station   and
      glanced at me
Dripping water   inexplicable   then we all grabbed hold like
      a tug-of-war.

We were gaining a little   from us a cry went up   from
      everywhere
People came running. Behind us the house filled with men and
      boys.
On the third step from the sea I took my place   looking down
      the rope
Going into the ocean, humming and shaking off drops. A
      houseful
Of people put their backs into it   going up the steps from me
Into the living room   through the kitchen   down the back
      stairs
Up and over a hill of sand   across a dust road   and onto a
      raised field
Of dunes   we were gaining   the rope in my hands began to
      be wet

With deeper water   all other haulers retreated through the
       house
But Payton and I on the stairs   drawing hand over hand on
       our blood
Drawing into existence by the nose   a huge body   becoming
A hammerhead   rolling in beery shadows   and I began to
       let up
But the rope still strained behind me   the town had gone
Pulling mad in our house: far away in a field of sand they
       struggled
They had turned their backs on the sea   bent double   some
       on their knees
The rope over their shoulders like a bag of gold   they strove
       for the ideal
Esso station across the scorched meadow   with the distant fish
       coming up
The front stairs   the sagging boards   still coming in   up
       taking
Another step towards the empty house   where the rope stood
       straining
By itself through the rooms   in the middle of the air. 'Pass the
       word,'
Payton said, and I screamed it: 'Let up, good God, let up!' to
       no one there.
The shark flopped on the porch, grating with salt-sand   driving
       back in
The nails he had pulled out   coughing chunks of his formless
       blood.
The screen door banged and tore off   he scrambled on his
       tail   slid
Curved   did a thing from another world,   and was out of his
       element and in
Our vacation paradise   cutting all four legs from under the
       dinner table
With one deep-water move   he unwove the rugs in a moment
       throwing pints
Of blood over everything we owned   knocked the buck teeth
       out of my picture.
His odd head full of crushed jelly-glass splinters and radio tubes
       thrashing
Among the pages of fan magazines   all the movie stars
       drenched in sea-blood.

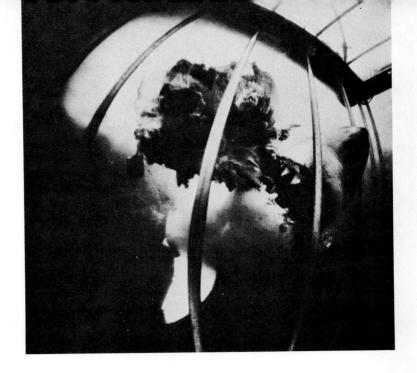

Each time we thought he was dead   he struggled back and smashed
One more thing   in all coming back to die   three or four
    more times after death.
At last we got him out   log-rolling him   greasing his
    sandpaper skin
With lard to slide him   pulling on his chained lips as the tide
    came
Tumbled him down the steps as the first night wave went under
    the floor.
He drifted off   head back   belly white as the moon. What
    could I do but buy
That house   for the one black mark still there against death
    a forehead-toucher in the room he circles beneath   and
    has been invited to wreck?
Blood hard as iron on the wall   black with time   still
    bloodlike
Can be touched whenever the brow is drunk enough: all
    changes: Memory.

JAMES DICKEY

Trapped

Night was falling. The sun was sinking into the sea, casting a great wide red arc of light over the calm water. The cliffs that had looked grey during the daytime were now black and their faces seemed to ooze water, a sort of perspiration that pours from them during the night. Beneath them the sea was a deep, deep blue, almost black, and the little waves never broke at all but swelled in and out murmuring. It was very beautiful, silent and dreamy.

Bartly Hernon the bird-catcher had descended the cliff-path from the summit of the Clogher Mor and landed on the broad plateau that protrudes from the face of the cliff, about fifty feet above the level of the sea. To the left the cliffs curved inwards, forming a half-circle. They bellied out far over their concave bases. There were great wide clefts in them, like scars running horizontally between each massive layer of stone that formed the foundation of the earth above them. From the plateau the great height of the cliffs made the fissures look small, but a man could stand erect in some of them. And the little stones, that could be seen wedged in their mouths here and there, were really huge boulders, buttressing the upper lairs of the cliffs.

Hernon was a very big man with finely developed limbs and a square muscular head. His face was tanned brown by the elements and great strong fair hairs covered the backs of his hands. He was all fairhaired and his face had the gentle, passive expression of the man who never thinks of anything but physical things. An ever-active, fearless man, he was so used to the danger of climbing the cliffs that he was as surefooted as a goat. He carried a sack, a heavy short stick and a small basket. The sack was to carry the birds. The stick was used to club them. He stored the eggs in the basket.

In order to reach the entrance to the lower fissure, one he was to explore that night, he had to scale a very narrow and difficult path along the cliff face for a distance of about twenty yards. This path was formed by a portion of the cliff coming loose and slanting out at an angle of ten degrees or so from the cliff itself. It looked like a crazy structure of boxes, piled one on top of the other irregularly. It seemed that one had only to give it a slight push and it would topple over into the sea. About five hundred tons of stone. Between the cliff face and this slanting pile, loose rocks had fallen. Along these rocks Hernon had to go. He had been many times through this pass, and it had never occurred to him that there was any danger in it. The broken pile had been there as long as anyone in the district could remember. It had a name and it was part of the country. So it would always be there. If it fell it would be impossible to reach those fissures where the sea-birds lived, or, having reached them, to get back to the plateau. But among our peasants it was unmanly even to think of its being dangerous to go up that way.

Hernon took off his shoes and left them on the rock. He also took off his frieze waistcoat and left it with his shoes. He would leave them there until his return in the morning. He took a piece of the bread which he carried in a red handkerchief and ate it. The remainder he placed beside the waistcoat. If he got hungry during the night, very hungry, he could suck a raw rockbird's egg. It was very strong but very good to prevent that sort of hunger-sickness which men get sometimes in the cliffs; not from hunger but begotten of the terrific solitude and darkness of the caverns. The remainder of the bread he would eat in the morning, on his return, before climbing to the cliff-top.

He tightened his belt and began to climb. All those big rocks were loose and very smooth. He had to jump from one to another, gripping for footholds with his hands and toes, crouching like a dancer and then jumping, curled up in a ball, so that he landed on all fours. He got almost to the end of the pass when he missed his foothold. He swayed for a moment out over the sea. Then he gasped and swung himself in towards the cliff, grasping a pointed rock that projected. The rock held his weight until he reached another foothold in the entrance to the fissure. Then as he strained at it further to raise himself and thrust himself forward, it gave way with a rumbling noise. Terrified at finding the rock coming loose with his hands, he hurled himself forward on his face and clung to the wet floor of the fissure. He lay still.

It was the first time he had missed a foothold scaling that pass, and he was stupefied with terror. It always happens that way with a fearless man who has done daring things but has never met with an accident. He listened without looking behind him.

There was a dull rumble as the loosened rock fell with a thud against the slanting pile. Then there was silence for about half a second. Then the silence was broken by a slight snapping sound like the end of a dog's yawn. That sound changed into another and louder one, as of a soft mound bursting. Yet nothing seemed to move; until suddenly there was a tremendous crash. A cloud of dust rose in the air and the great pile of broken cliff hurtled down to the sea, casting rocks far out into the dark waters, where they fell with a pattering sound, while the bulk subsided to the base of the cliff and became still almost immediately. When the cloud of dust cleared away the face of the cliff was again smooth and unbroken. There was not a foothold for a cat from the fissure at whose entrance Hernon lay to the plateau beyond. It was a distance of twenty yards, past a hump in the cliff. Hernon was trapped.

He was perspiring. He turned his head and looked behind. When he saw the smooth face of the cliff, where a minute before there had been a pile of loose rocks and a path, his mouth opened wide and his look became fixed. 'Jesus, Mary and Joseph,' he said. He remained motionless for over a minute staring at the smooth, dark-grey bulging face of the cliff that cut off his return. He kept staring at it stupidly, as if expecting that the pile of rock would rise again and cover it. But the only thing that happened was that tiny rivulets of water oozed from it and began to descend slowly, dropping down to the sea, just like the rest of the cliff. It almost immediately looked old like the remainder of the cliff, as if it had been shaped that way for centuries.

'You horned devil,' muttered Hernon, suddenly becoming terrified of it and crawling away up the fissure on his hands and knees. The fissure was very low at its entrance. But it rapidly widened so that after ten yards or so, a man could walk in it, stooping slightly to avoid an occasional boss of stone that jutted down from the roof. Hernon, however, was so stupefied that he kept crawling, long after he had passed the narrow strip, until he bumped his head against a boulder that propped up the roof. Then he jumped up and looked around him wildly.

Night had completely fallen within the caverns. It was pitch-black. But looking out to sea over the edge of the cliff, he could still see the water and the sky lit up by the twilight. He sat down on the rock to recover from his shock and plan some means of escape. But instead of concentrating on how he was to escape he kept remembering all the men in the district who had been killed in the cliffs: Brian Derrane, who fell from the top of a cliff while hunting a rabbit; John Halloran, who got entangled in a fishing-line he was swinging out and got carried out with it; and several others. Gradually he felt a curious longing to look out over the edge of the cliff and throw himself down.

He was not aware of the desire to throw himself down until he bent forward and looked down. It was about one hundred feet to the sea. He could distinguish the forms of large boulders in the tide and flat rocks with seaweed growing on them. And as he looked at them he felt a sudden desire to hurl himself down. That terrified him. He jumped up and crawled back, until he pressed his body against the back of the cavern. He was quite helpless with fear now.

He lay there for a long time quite motionless. It was pitch-dark now. All sorts of sea-birds were flying in and out. The whirring of their wings in the darkness was a terrifying sound, because they were invisible and they did not scream. They were all returning to their nesting-places for the night, in the interminable holes in the fissure. Hernon took no notice of this sound because he was used to it. Afterwards, when the moon rose and the place was lit up with a yellow light, he had intended to prowl among the caverns and club the sleeping birds. But now he was not thinking of the birds but of death.

It is extraordinary that physically fearless men like Hernon are always thrown into a panic like this when confronted by something they cannot understand. They are always eager to face danger when they can see it and understand its nature and touch it physically. But I have always noticed among our peasants that these rough, strong, unthinking men like Hernon are quite hopeless in a situation that demands thought if they have no one to guide them. Whereas the small, weak, cunning types of peasant, who invariably avoid danger, are always subtle and resourceful when placed in a dangerous position.

But very probably the danger of his position had been discussed beforehand around the village firesides, as is the custom on winter evenings, and he understood the hopelessness of it. It was absolutely impossible to reach the summit of the cliff. It was two hundred feet away and it bellied out, so that even if people came with a rope, the rope would dangle twenty feet away from him, absolutely out of reach. And it was equally impossible to throw a rope from the sea, up a distance of one hundred feet.

At last the moon rose. Gradually the yellow light lit up the sea, the cliffs and the caverns. It was very weird but it revived Hernon. He was quite used to the moonlight in the cliffs. It was something physical that he could understand. The birds were now all asleep and there was perfect silence.

He got up and began to walk along the edge of the precipice, looking down and examining its face, seeking a path to descend. Even if he could get down to the sea he would have to swim over a mile in the night before he could get a landing-place, and there were sharks in the water. But he could not wait till morning, until perhaps a boat might come looking for him. He was too panic-stricken to wait.

The fissure, in which he was, wound irregularly through the face of the cliff for a distance of almost half a mile. But here and there it was so narrow that there was only a tiny ledge, a few inches wide, leading from one deep cavern to another. These passes were very dangerous even in broad daylight. But Hernon thought nothing of them. He had stopped crawling now. He dashed along, taking great bounds over pools, gripping the face of the cliff and swinging himself out over the edge of the cliff to reach another ledge. His figure, bending and bounding, looked wonderfully agile and beautiful in the half-darkness of the pale yellow moonlight; the mysterious bounding figure of a cliff-man. He had dropped his basket, his club and his sack. He had lost his cap. His fair hair shimmered in the mysterious moonlight.

Although he had been panic-stricken when he was crouching under the cliffs, he was now perfectly composed physically. His limbs moved instinctively although somewhere in the back of his mind there was the picture of a skeleton that had once been found in these caverns. Some man, years ago, had been wedged in among boulders at the back of a cavern and had died there, unable to extricate himself. That was a legend. It drove him on. But his body was cool and his limbs acted methodically, moving with supple ease, performing amazing feats of agility.

However, he went along several hundred yards without seeing the least sign of a path down to the sea. Then at last he turned a corner and came to a place called the Cormorants' Bed. Here there was an enormous cavern. Down from it to the sea there was a big black crack in the cliff. The cliff face was as smooth as elsewhere, but there was a long, straight stone, pointed like a wedge, running straight down. Hernon looked at it and wondered could he grip it with his knees and slide down slowly. His forehead wrinkled and he shuddered thinking of it. He looked down. There were rocks at the bottom. He would be smashed to pieces if he lost his hold. Yet without pausing he moved towards the cavern. He rounded a very narrow ledge and stumbled into a pool at the entrance to the cavern. Immediately there was a wild screech and hundreds of great black figures whirred past his head, flapping their wings. He stooped to avoid them, because these birds, going past on the wing, could knock him over the edge of the precipice. Then when they had passed he groped his way to the wedge-shaped rock that ran down. He made the sign of the cross on his forehead, rubbed his palms together, grunted and stiffened himself. Then he gripped the rock savagely, swung his body around it and gripped with his knees. He hung on to it for a moment, like an animal crouched on its prey. Then he began to descend.

As soon as he moved downwards, he was seized with dizziness. His limbs shivered and he almost lost his hold. A prickly sensation went through his body to his heart, like a prod from a needle. But in an instant he stiffened himself and held his breath. The fit passed and he ceased to be conscious. His limbs moved mechanically and his eyes stared unseeingly at the wedge-shaped rock that he held. He went down and down inch by inch, each muscle rigid, moving with the slow, awkward movement of a bear, his broad back bent, his neck muscles cracking with the strain on his spine. His skin was perfectly dry, as if all the perspiration had been drained from the pores.

Then at last he found himself sitting on a rock at the bottom of the cliff. He still clung to the cliff, pawing at it, for several moments before he became aware that he had reached the bottom. When he did become aware of it he uttered a loud oath, 'You horned devil,' and then perspiration stood out on his forehead once more.

But curiously enough, it was not through fear he was perspiring, but through pride. He had done a mighty thing. He had descended where no man ever had descended. Exalted with joy and pride, he waved his hand over his head and uttered a wild yell. The sound re-echoed again and again among the caverns of the cliffs, and before it died, thousands of sea-birds rushed from their ledges screaming. The air was full of terrifying sound. Hernon jumped from the rock where he still sat and, without pausing, plunged into the sea, terrified once more by the eerie sounds in the devilish caverns from which he had escaped.

The sea was dead calm, shimmering under the moonlight that fell on it, making a broad silver path with golden rims, while afar it faded into blackness under a starlit pale sky. On a level with the sea, the cliffs seemed to reach the sky. The sea appeared to be walled in by them, like water in a deep basin. Afar off on the left there was a sharp promontory where the cliffs ended. Beyond that there was a rocky beach below the village. That was where Hernon could land. It was over a mile.

He began to swim with all his strength, swimming on his side, heaving through the water with a rushing sound like a swan. He was a great swimmer. His beautiful muscular shoulders rose out of the water, his long arm shot out circularly, he thrust forward his other arm like a sword-thrust and then he heaved forward, churning with his feet, while he shook his head and spat the brine from his panting mouth. In the water he was conscious of no danger. All his muscles were in action and he saw the open sea before him to traverse. In spite of his terrific exertion in the cliff and descending, he was quite fresh and he never slackened speed until he passed the promontory. Then he turned over on his back and let himself be carried in by the

great rolling waves that drive to the rocky
beach. Then he turned once more on his
chest and swam to the low weed-covered
rock on which row-boats landed. He
mounted the rock and waded on to dry
land. He was safe. He rushed up the
shore and knelt on the pebbles.
Crossing himself, he began
to pray aloud, thanking
God. But while he prayed
he kept thinking of
what the village
people would say
of his heroic feat.

LIAM O'FLAHERTY

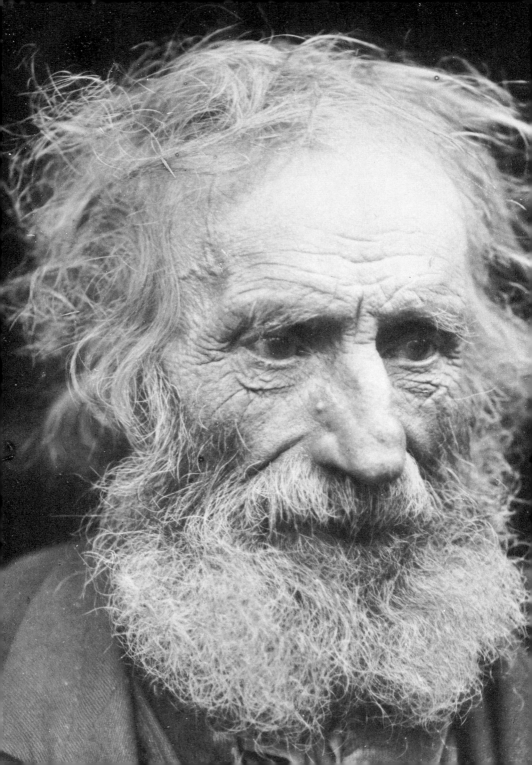

Sunday

Michael marched off to chapel beside his sister, rapping his Sunday shoes down on to the pavement to fetch the brisk, stinging echo off housewalls, wearing the detestable blue blazer with its meaningless badge as a uniform loaded with honours and privilege. In chapel he sat erect, arms folded, instead of curling down on to his spine like a prawn and sinking his chin between his collar-bones as under the steady pressure of a great hand, which was his usual attitude of worship. He sang the hymns and during the prayers thought exultantly of Top Wharf Pub, trying to remember what time those places opened.

All this zest, however, was no match for the sermon. The minister's voice soared among the beams, tireless, as if he were still rehearsing, and after ten minutes these organ-like modulations began to work Michael into a torment of impatience. The nerve-ends all over his body prickled and swarmed. He almost had to sink to his knees. Thoughts of shouting, 'Oh, well!' – one enormous sigh, or simply running out of chapel, brought a fine sweat on to his temples. Finally he closed his eyes and began to imagine a wolf galloping through snow-filled, moonlit forest. Without fail this image was the first thing in his mind whenever he shut his eyes on these situations of constraint, in school, in waiting-rooms, with visitors. The wolf urged itself with all its strength through a land empty of everything but trees and snow. After a while he drifted to vaguer things, a few moments of freedom before his impatience jerked him back to see how the sermon was going. It was still soaring. He closed his eyes and the wolf was there again.

By the time the doors opened, letting light stream in, he felt stupefied. He edged out with the crowd. Then the eleven-o'clock Sunday sky struck him. He had forgotten it was so early in the day. But with the light and the outside world his mind returned in a rush. Leaving his sister deep in the chapel, buried in a pink and blue bouquet of her friends, and evading the minister who, having processed his congregation generally within, had darted round the side of the chapel to the porch and was now setting his personal seal, a crushing smile and a soft, supporting handclasp, on each member of the flock as they stumbled out, Michael took the three broad steps at a leap and dodged down the crowded path among the graves, like a person with an important dispatch.

But he was no sooner out through the gate than the stitches of his shoes seemed suddenly to tighten, and his damped hair tightened on his scalp. He slowed to a walk.

To the farthest skyline it was Sunday. The valley walls, throughout the week wet, hanging, uncomfortable woods and mud-hole farms, were today neat, remote, and irreproachably pretty, postcard pretty. The blue sky, the sparklingly smokeless Sunday air, had disinfected them. Picnickers and chapel-hikers were already up there, sprinkled like confetti along the steep lanes and paths, creeping imperceptibly upward towards the brown line of the moors. Spotless, harmless, church-going slopes! Life, over the whole countryside, was suspended for the day.

Below him the town glittered in the clear air and sunlight. Throughout the week it resembled from this point a volcanic pit, bottomless in places, a jagged fissure into a sulphurous underworld, the smoke dragging off the chimneys of the mills and houserows like a tearing fleece. Now it lay as under shallow, slightly warm, clear water, with still streets and bright yards.

There was even something Sundayish about the pavements, something untouchably proper, though nothing had gone over them since grubby Saturday except more feet and darkness.

Superior to all this for once, and quite enjoying it again now he was on his way, Michael went down the hill into the town with strides that jammed his toes into the ends of his shoes. He turned into the Memorial Gardens, past prams, rockeries, forbidden grass, trees with labels, and over the ornamental canal bridge to the bowling greens that lay on the level between canal and river.

His father was there, on the farthest green, with two familiar figures – Harry Rutley, the pork butcher, and Mr Stinson, a tall, sooty, lean man who held his head as if he were blind and spoke rarely, and then only as if phrasing his most private thoughts to himself. A man Michael preferred not to look at. Michael sat on a park bench behind their jack and tried to make himself obvious.

The paths were full of people. Last night this had been a parade of couples, foursomes, gangs and lonely ones – the electricity gathered off looms, sewing-machines and shop counters since Monday milling round the circuit and discharging up the side-paths among the shrubbery in giggling darkness and shrieks. But now it was families, an after-chapel procession of rustlings and murmurings, lacy bosoms, tight blue pinstripe suits and daisy-chains of children. Soon Michael was worn out, willing the bowls against their bias or against the crown of the green or to roll one foot farther and into the trough or to collide and fall in halves.

He could see the Wesleyan Church clock at quarter past eleven and stared at it for what seemed like five minutes, convinced it had stopped.

He stood up as the three men came over to study the pattern of the bowls.

'Are we going now, Dad?'

'Just a minute, lad. Come and have a game.'

That meant at least another game whether he played or not. Another quarter of an hour! And to go and get out a pair of bowls was as good as agreeing to stay there playing till one.

'We might miss him.'

His father laughed. Only just remembering his promise, thought Michael.

'He'll not be there till well on. We shan't miss him.'

His father kicked his bowls together and Harry Rutley slewed the rubber mat into position.

'But will he be there sure?'

Sunday dinner was closer every minute. Then it was sleepy Sunday afternoon. Then Aunt-infested Sunday tea. His father laughed again.

'Billy Red'll be coming down today, won't he, Harry?'

Harry Rutley, pale, slow, round, weighed his jack. He had lost the tip of an ear at the Dardanelles and carried a fragment of his fifth rib on the end of his watch-chain. Now he narrowed his eyes, choosing a particular blade of grass on the far corner of the green.

'Billy Red? Every Sunday. Twelve on the dot.' He dipped his body to the underswing of his arm and came upright as the jack curled away across the green. 'I don't know how he does it.'

The jack had come to rest two feet from the far corner. There followed four more games. They played back to Michael, then across to the far right, then a short one down to the far left, then back to the near right. At last the green was too full, with nine or ten games interweaving and shouts of 'feet' every other minute and bowls bocking together in mid-green.

At quarter to twelve on the clock – Michael now sullen with the punishment he had undergone and the certainty that his day had been played away – the three men came off the green, put away their bowls, and turned down on to the canal bank towpath.

The valley became narrower and its sides steeper. Road, river and canal made their way as best they could, with only a twenty-yard strip of wasteland – a tangle of rank weeds, elderberry bushes and rubble, bleached debris of floods – separating river and canal. Along the far side of the river squeezed the road, rumbling from Monday to Saturday with swaying lorry-loads of cotton and wool and cloth. The valley wall on that side, draped with a network of stone-walled fields and precariously-clinging farms and woods, came down sheer out of the sky into the backyards of a crouched stone row of weavers' cottages whose front doorsteps were almost part of the road. The river ran noisily over pebbles. On the strip of land between river and canal stood Top Wharf Pub – its buildings tucked in under the bank of the canal so that the towpath ran level with the back bedroom windows. On this side the valley wall, with over-shadowing woods, dived straight into the black, motionless canal as if it must be a mile deep. The water was quite shallow, however, with its collapsed banks and accumulation of mud, so shallow that in some places the rushes grew right across. For years it had brought nothing to Top Wharf Pub but a black greasy damp and rats.

They turned down off the towpath into the wide, cobbled yard in front of the pub.

'You sit here. Now what would you like to drink?'

Michael sat on the cracked, weather-scrubbed bench in the yard under the bar-room window and asked for ginger beer.

'And see if he's come yet. And see if they have any rats ready.'

He had begun to notice the heat and now leaned back against the wall to get the last slice of shade under the eaves. But in no time the sun had moved out over the yard. The valley sides funnelled its rays down as into a trap, dazzling the quartz-points of the worn cobbles, burning the colour off everything. The flies were going wild, swirling in the air, darting and basking on the cobbles – big, green-glossed blue-bottles that leapt on to his hand when he laid it along the hot bench.

In twos and threes men came over the hog-backed bridge leading from the road into the yard, or down off the towpath. Correct, leisurely and a little dazed from morning service, or in overalls that were torn and whitened from obscure Sabbath labours, all dis-appeared through the door. The hubbub inside thickened. Michael strained to catch some mention of Billy Red.

At last his father brought him his ginger beer and informed him that Billy Red had not arrived yet but everybody was expecting him and he shouldn't be long. They had some nice rats ready.

In spite of the heat, Michael suddenly did not feel like drinking. His whole body seemed to have become frailer and slightly faint, as with hunger. When he sipped, the liquid trickled with a cold, tasteless weight into his disinterested stomach.

He left the glass on the bench and went to the Gents. Afterwards he walked stealthily round the yard, looking in at the old stables and coach-house, the stony cave silences. Dust, cobwebs, rat droppings. Old timbers, old wheels, old harness. Barrels, and rusty stoves. He listened for rats. Walking back across the blinding, humming yard he smelt roast beef and heard the clattering of the pub kitchen and saw through the open window fat arms working over a stove. The whole world was at routine Sunday dinner. The potatoes were already steaming, people sitting about killing time and getting impatient and wishing that something would fall out of the blue and knowing that nothing would. The idea stifled him, he didn't want to think of it. He went quickly back to the bench and sat down, his heart beating as if he had run.

A car nosed over the little bridge and stopped at the far side of the yard, evidently not sure whether it was permitted to enter the yard at all. Out of it stepped a well-to-do young man and a young woman. The young man unbuttoned his pale tweed jacket, thrust his hands into his trouser pockets and came sauntering towards the pub door, the girl on her high heels following beside him, patting her hair and looking round at the scenery as if she had just come up out of a dark pit. They stood at the door for a moment, improvising their final decisions about what she would drink, whether this was the right place, and whether she ought to come in. He was sure it was the right place, this was where they did it all right, and he motioned her to sit on the end of the bench beside Michael. Michael moved accommodatingly to the other end. She ignored him, however, and perched on the last ten inches of the bench, arrayed her wide-skirted, summery, blue-flowered frock over her knees, and busied herself with her mirror. The flies whirled around, inspecting this new thing of scents.

Suddenly there came a shout from the doorway of the pub, long drawn words: 'Here comes the man.'

Immediately several crowded to the doorway, glasses in their hands.

'Here he comes.'

'The Red Killer!'

'Poor little beggar. He looks as if he lives on rat meat.'

'Draw him a half, Gab.'

Over the bridge and into the yard shambled a five-foot, ragged figure. Scarecrowish, tawny to colourless, exhausted, this was Billy Red, the rat-catcher. As a sideline he kept hens, and he had something of the raw, flea-bitten look of a red hen, with his small, sunken features and gingery hair. From the look of his clothes you would think he slept on the hen-house floor, under the roosts. One hand in his pocket, his back at a half-bend, he drifted aimlessly to a stop. Then, to show that after all he had only come for a sit in the sun, he sat down beside Michael with a long sigh.

'It's a grand day,' he announced. His voice was not strong – lungless, a shaky wisp, full of hen-fluff and dust.

Michael peered closely and secretly at this wrinkled, neglected fifty-year-old face shrunk on its small skull. Among the four-day stubble and enlarged pores and deep folds it was hard to make out anything, but there were one or two marks that might have been old rat bites. He had a little withered mouth and kept moving the lips about as if he couldn't get them comfortable. After a sigh he would pause a minute, leaning forward, one elbow on his knees, then sigh again, changing his position, the other elbow now on the other knee, like a man too weary to rest.

'Here you are, Billy.'

A hand held a half-pint high at the pub door like a sign and with startling readiness Billy leapt to his feet and disappeared into the pub, gathering the half-pint on the way and saying:

'I've done a daft bloody thing. I've come down all this way wi'out money brass.'

There was an obliging roar of laughter and Michael found himself looking at the girl's powdered profile. She was staring down at her neatly-covered toe as it twisted this way and that, presenting all its polished surfaces.

Things began to sound livelier inside – sharp, loud remarks kicking up bursts of laughter and showering exclamations. The young man came out, composed, serious, and handed the girl a long-stemmed clear glass with a cherry in it. He sat down between her and Michael, splaying his knees as he did so and lunging his face forward to meet his streamingly raised pint – one smooth, expert motion.

'He's in there now,' he said, wiping his mouth. 'They're getting him ready.'

The girl gazed into his face, tilting her glass till the cherry bobbed against her pursed red lips, opening her eyes wide.

Michael looked past her to the doorway. A new figure had appeared. He supposed this must be the landlord, Gab – an aproned hemisphere and round, red greasy face that screwed itself up to survey the opposite hillside.

'Right,' called the landlord. 'I'll get 'em.' Away he went, wiping his hands on his apron, then letting them swing wide of his girth like penguin flippers, towards the coach-house. Now everybody came out of the pub and Michael stood up, surprised to see how many had been crowded in there. They were shouting and laughing, pausing to browse their pints, circulating into scattered groups. Michael went over and stood beside his father who was one of an agitated four. He had to ask twice before he could make himself heard. Even to himself his voice sounded thinner than usual, empty, as if at bottom it wanted nothing so much as to dive into his stomach and hide there in absolute silence, letting events go their own way.

'How many is he going to do?'

'I think they've got two.' His father half turned down towards him. 'It's usually two or three.'

Nobody took any notice of Billy Red who was standing a little apart, his hands hanging down from the slight stoop that seemed more or less permanent with him, smiling absently at the noisy, hearty groups. He brightened and straightened as the last man out of the pub came across, balancing a brimming pint glass. Michael watched. The moment the pint touched those shrivelled lips the pale little eye set with a sudden strangled intentness. His long, skinny, unshaven throat writhed and the beer shrank away in the glass. In two or three seconds he lowered the glass empty, wiped his mouth on his sleeve and looked around. Then as nobody stepped forward to offer him a fill-up he set the glass down to the cobbles and stood drying his hands on his jacket.

Michael's gaze shifted slightly, and he saw the girl. He recognized his own thoughts in her look of mesmerized incredulity. At her side the young man was watching too, but shrewdly, between steady drinks.

The sun seemed to have come to a stop directly above. Two or three men had taken their jackets off, with irrelevant, noisy clowning, a few sparring feints. Somebody suggested they all go and stand in the canal and Billy Red do his piece under water, and another laughed so hard at this that the beer came spurting from his nostrils. High up on the opposite slope Michael could see a line of Sunday walkers, moving slowly across the dazed grey of the fields. Their coats would be over their shoulders, their ties in their pockets, their shoes agony, the girls asking to be pushed – but if they stood quite still they would feel a breeze. In the cobbled yard the heat had begun to dance.

'Here we are.'

The landlord waddled into the middle of the yard holding up an oblong wire cage. He set it down with a clash on the cobbles.

'Two of the best.'

Everybody crowded round. Michael squeezed to the front and crouched down beside the cage. There was a pause of admiration. Hunched in opposite corners of the cage, their heads low and drawn in and their backs pressed to the wires so that the glossy black-tipped hairs bristled out, were two big brown rats. They sat quiet. A long pinkish-grey tail, thick at the root as his thumb, coiled out by Michael's foot. He touched the hairy tip of it gently with his forefinger.

'Watch out, lad!'

The rat snatched its tail in, leapt across the cage with a crash and gripping one of the zinc bars behind its curved yellow teeth, shook till the cage rattled. The other rat left its corner and began gliding to and fro along one side – a continuous low fluidity, sniffing up and down the bars. Then both rats stopped and sat up on their hind-legs, like persons coming out of a trance, suddenly recognizing people. Their noses quivered as they directed their set, grey-chinned inquisitive expressions at one face after another.

The landlord had been loosening the nooses in the end of two long pieces of dirty string. He lifted the cage again.

'Catch a tail, Walt.'

The group pressed closer. A hand came out and roamed in readiness under the high-held cage floor. The rats moved uneasily. The landlord gave the cage a shake and the rats crashed. A long tail swung down between the wires. The hand grabbed and pulled.

'Hold it.'

The landlord slipped the noose over the tail, down to the very butt, and pulled it tight. The caught rat, not quite convinced before but now understanding the whole situation, doubled round like a thing without bones, and bit and shook the bars and forced its nose out between them to get at the string that held its buttocks tight to the cage side.

'Just you hold that string, Walt. So's it can't get away when we open up.'

Now the landlord lifted the cage again, while Walt held his string tight. The other rat, watching the operation on its companion, had bunched up in a corner, sitting on its tail.

'Clever little beggar. You know what I'm after, don't you?'

The landlord gave the cage a shake, but the rat clung on, its pink feet gripping the wires of the cage floor like hands. He shook the cage violently.

'Move, you stubborn little beggar,' demanded the landlord. He went on shaking the cage with sharp, jerking movements.

Then the rat startled everybody. Squeezing still farther into its corner, it opened its mouth wide and began to scream – a harsh, ripping, wavering scream travelling out over the yard like some thin, metallic, dazzling substance that decomposed instantly. As one scream died the rat started another, its mouth wide. Michael had never thought a rat could make so much noise. As it went on at full intensity, his stomach began to twist and flex like a thick muscle. For a moment he was so worried by these sensations that he stopped looking at the rat. The landlord kept on shaking the cage and the scream shook in the air, but the rat clung on, still sitting on its tail.

'Give him a poke, Gab, stubborn little beggar!'

The landlord held the cage still, reached into his top pocket and produced a pencil. At this moment, Michael saw the girl, extricating herself from the press, pushing out backwards. The ring of rapt faces and still legs closed again. The rat was hurtling round the cage, still screaming, leaping over the other, attacking the wires first at this side then at that. All at once it crouched in a corner, silent. A hand came out and grabbed the loop of tail. The other noose was there ready. The landlord set the cage down.

Now the circle relaxed and everyone looked down at the two rats flattened on the cage bottom, their tails waving foolishly outside the wires.

'Well then, Billy,' said the landlord. 'How are they?'

Billy Red nodded and grinned.

'Them's grand,' he said. 'Grand.' His little rustling voice made Michael want to cough.

'Right. Stand back.'

Everybody backed obediently, leaving the cage, Walt with his foot on one taut string and the landlord with his foot on the other in the middle of an arena six or seven yards across. Michael saw the young man on the far side, his glass still half full in his hand. The girl was nowhere to be seen.

Billy Red peeled his coat off, exposing an old shirt, army issue, most of the left arm missing. He pulled his trousers up under his belt, spat on his hands, and took up a position which placed the cage door a couple of paces or so from his left side and slightly in front of him. He bent forward a little more than usual, his arms hanging like a wary wrestler's, his eyes fixed on the cage.

'Eye like a bloody sparrow-hawk,' somebody murmured.

There was a silence. The landlord waited, kneeling now beside the cage. Nothing disturbed the dramatic moment but the distant, brainless church bells.

'This one first, Walt,' said the landlord. 'Ready, Billy?'

He pushed down the lever that raised the cage door and let his rat have its full five- or six-yard length of string. He had the end looped round his hand. Walt kept his rat on a tight string.

Everybody watched intently. The freed rat pulled its tail in delicately and sniffed at the noose round it, ignoring the wide-open door. Then the landlord reached to tap the cage and in a flash the rat vanished.

Michael lost sight of it. But he saw Billy Red spin half round and drop smack down on his hands and knees on the cobbles.

'He's got it!'

Billy Red's face was compressed in a snarl and as he snapped his head from side to side the dark, elongated body of the rat whipped around his neck. He had it by the shoulders. Michael's eyes fixed like cameras.

A dozen shakes, and Billy Red stopped, his head lowered. The rat hanging from his mouth was bunching and relaxing, bunching and relaxing. He waited. Everyone waited. Then the rat spasmed, fighting with all its paws, and Billy shook again wildly, the rat's tail flying like a lash. This time when he stopped the body hung down limply. The piece of string, still attached to the tail, trailed away across the cobbles.

Gently Billy took the rat from his mouth and laid it down. He stood up, spat a couple of times, and began to wipe his mouth, smiling shamefacedly. Everybody breathed out – an exclamation of marvelling disgust and admiration, and loud above the rest:

'Pint now, Billy?'

The landlord walked back into the pub and most of the audience followed him to refresh their glasses. Billy Red stood separate, still wiping his mouth with a scrap of snuff-coloured cloth.

Michael went over and bent to look at the dead rat. Its shoulders were wet-black with saliva, and the fur bitten. It lay on its left side, slightly curved, its feet folded, its eyes still round and bright in their alert, inquisitive expression. He touched its long, springy whiskers. A little drip of blood was puddling under its nose on the cobblestones. As he watched, a bluebottle alighted on its tail and sprang off again, then suddenly reappeared on its nose, inspecting the blood.

He walked over to the cage. Walt was standing there talking, his foot on the taut string. This rat crouched against the wires as if they afforded some protection. It made no sign of noticing Michael as he bent low over it. Its black beads stared outward fixedly, its hot brown flanks going in and out. There was a sparkle on its fur, and as he looked more closely, thinking it must be perspiration, he became aware of the heat again.

He stood up, a dull pain in his head. He put his hand to his scalp and pressed the scorch down into his skull, but that didn't seem to connect with the dull, thick pain.

'I'm off now, Dad,' he called.

'Already? Aren't you going to see this other one?'

'I think I'll go.' He set off across the yard.

'Finish your drink,' his father called after him.

He saw his glass almost full on the end of the white bench but walked past it and round the end of the pub and up on to the towpath. The sycamore trees across the canal arched over black damp shade and the still water. High up, the valley slopes were silvered now, frizzled with the noon brightness. The earthen towpath was like stone. Fifty yards along he passed the girl in the blue-flowered frock sauntering back towards the pub, pulling at the heads of the tall bank grasses.

'Have they finished yet?' she asked.

Michael shook his head. He found himself unable to speak. With all his strength he began to run.

TED HUGHES

The celebrated Dog BILLY killin...

Design'd & etch'd by Theodore Lane

...0 Rats at the Westminster Pit

& Lacey July 1 1825

139

The Peacelike Mongoose

In cobra country a mongoose was born one day who didn't want to fight cobras or anything else. The word spread from mongoose to mongoose that there was a mongoose who didn't want to fight cobras. If he didn't want to fight anything else, it was his own business, but it was the duty of every mongoose to kill cobras or be killed by cobras.

'Why?' asked the peacelike mongoose, and the word went round that the strange new mongoose was not only pro-cobra and anti-mongoose but intellectually curious and against the ideals and traditions of mongoosism.

'He is crazy,' cried the young mongoose's father.

'He is sick,' said his mother.

'He is a coward,' shouted his brothers.

'He is a mongoosexual,' whispered his sisters.

Strangers who had never laid eyes on the peacelike mongoose remembered that they had seen him crawling on his stomach, or trying on cobra hoods, or plotting the violent overthrow of Mongoosia.

'I am trying to use reason and intelligence,' said the strange new mongoose.

'Reason is six-sevenths of treason,' said one of his neighbours.

'Intelligence is what the enemy uses,' said another.

Finally the rumour spread that the mongoose had venom in his sting, like a cobra, and he was tried, convicted by a show of paws, and condemned to banishment.

Moral: Ashes to ashes, and clay to clay, if the enemy doesn't get you your own folks may.

JAMES THURBER

Manhood

Swiftly free-wheeling, their breath coming easily, the man and the boy steered their bicycles down the short dip which led them from woodland into open country. Then they looked ahead and saw that the road began to climb.

'Now, Rob,' said Mr Willison, settling his plump haunches firmly on the saddle, 'just up that rise and we'll get off and have a good rest.'

'Can't we rest now?' the boy asked. 'My legs feel all funny. As if they're turning to water.'

'Rest at the top,' said Mr Willison firmly. 'Remember what I told you? The first thing any athlete has to learn is to break the fatigue barrier.'

'I've broken it already. I was feeling tired when we were going along the main road and I –'

'When fatigue sets in, the thing to do is to keep going until it wears off. Then you get your second wind and your second endurance.'

'I've already done that.'

'Up we go,' said Mr Willison, 'and at the top we'll have a good rest.' He panted slightly and stood on his pedals, causing his machine to sway from side to side in a laboured manner. Rob, falling silent, pushed doggedly at his pedals. Slowly, the pair wavered up the straight road to the top. Once there, Mr Willison dismounted with exaggerated steadiness, laid his bicycle carefully on its side, and spread his jacket on the ground before sinking down to rest. Rob slid hastily from the saddle and flung himself full-length on the grass.

'Don't lie there,' said his father. 'You'll catch cold.'

'I'm all right. I'm warm.'

'Come and sit on this. When you're over-heated, that's just when you're prone to –'

'I'm all *right*, Dad. I want to lie here. My back aches.'

'Your back needs strengthening, that's why it aches. It's a pity we don't live near a river where you could get some rowing.'

The boy did not answer, and Mr Willison, aware that he was beginning to sound like a nagging, over-anxious parent, allowed himself to be defeated and did not press the suggestion about Rob's coming to sit on his jacket. Instead, he waited a moment and then glanced at his watch.

'Twenty to twelve. We must get going in a minute.'

'*What?* I thought we were going to have a rest.'

141

'Well, we're having one, aren't we?' said Mr Willison reasonably. 'I've got my breath back, so surely you must have.'

'My back still aches. I want to lie here a bit.'

'Sorry,' said Mr Willison, getting up and moving over to his bicycle. 'We've got at least twelve miles to do and lunch is at one.'

'Dad, why did we have to come so far if we've got to get back for one o'clock? I know, let's find a telephone box and ring up Mum and tell her we –'

'Nothing doing. There's no reason why two fit men shouldn't cycle twelve miles in an hour and ten minutes.'

'But we've already done about a million miles.'

'We've done about fourteen, by my estimation,' said Mr Willison stiffly. 'What's the good of going for a bike ride if you don't cover a bit of distance?'

He picked up his bicycle and stood waiting. Rob, with his hand over his eyes, lay motionless on the grass. His legs looked thin and white among the rich grass.

'Come on, Rob.'

The boy showed no sign of having heard. Mr Willison got on to his bicycle and began to ride slowly away. 'Rob,' he called over his shoulder, 'I'm going.'

Rob lay like a sullen corpse by the roadside. He looked horribly like the victim of an accident, unmarked but dead from internal injuries. Mr Willison cycled fifty yards, then a hundred, then turned in a short, irritable circle and came back to where his son lay.

'Rob, is there something the matter or are you just being awkward?'

The boy removed his hand and looked up into his father's face. His eyes were surprisingly mild: there was no fire or rebellion in them.

'I'm tired and my back aches. I can't go on yet.'

'Look, Rob,' said Mr Willison gently, 'I wasn't going to tell you this, because I meant it to be a surprise, but when you get home you'll find a present waiting for you.'

'What kind of present?'

'Something very special I've bought for you. The man's coming this morning to fix it up. That's one reason why I suggested a bike ride this morning. He'll have done it by now.'

What is it?'

'Aha. It's a surprise. Come on, get on your bike and let's go home and see.'

Rob sat up, then slowly clambered to his feet. 'Isn't there a short cut home?'

'I'm afraid not. It's only twelve miles.'

Rob said nothing.

'And a lot of that's downhill,' Mr Willison added brightly. His own legs were tired and his muscles fluttered unpleasantly. In addition, he suddenly realized he was very thirsty. Rob, still without speaking, picked up his bicycle, and they pedalled away.

'Where is he?' Mrs Willison asked, coming into the garage.

'Gone up to his room,' said Mr Willison. He doubled his fist and gave the punch-ball a thudding blow. 'Seems to have fixed it pretty firmly. You gave him the instructions, I suppose.'

'What's he doing up in his room? It's lunch-time.'

'He said he wanted to rest a bit.'

'I hope you're satisfied,' said Mrs Willison. 'A lad of thirteen, nearly fourteen years of age, just when he should have a really big appetite, and when the lunch is put on the table he's *resting* –'

'Now look, I know what I'm –'

'Lying down in his room, resting, too tired to eat because you've dragged him up hill and down dale on one of your –'

'We did nothing that couldn't be reasonably expected of a boy of his age.'

'How do you know?' Mrs Willison demanded. 'You never did anything of that kind when you were a boy. How do you know what can be reasonably –'

'Now look,' said Mr Willison again. 'When I was a boy, it was study, study, study all the time, with the fear of unemployment and insecurity in everybody's mind. I was never even given a bicycle. I never boxed, I never rowed, I never did anything to develop my physique. It was just work, work, work, pass this exam, get that certificate. Well, I did it and now I'm qualified and in a secure job. But you know as well as I do that they let me down. Nobody encouraged me to build myself up.'

'Well, what does it matter? You're all right –'

'Grace!' Mr Willison interrupted sharply. 'I am not all right and you know it. I am under average height, my chest is flat and I'm –'

'What nonsense. You're taller than I am and I'm –'

'No son of mine is going to grow up with the same wretched physical heritage that I –'

'No, he'll just have heart disease through overtaxing his strength, because you haven't got the common sense to –'

'His heart is one hundred per cent all right. Not three weeks have gone by since the doctor looked at him.'

'Well, why does he get so over-tired if he's all right? Why is he lying down now instead of coming to the table, a boy of his age?'

A slender shadow blocked part of the dazzling sun in the door-way. Looking up simultaneously, the Willisons greeted their son.

'Lunch ready, Mum? I'm hungry.'

'Ready when you are,' Grace Willison beamed. 'Just wash your hands and come to the table.'

'Look, Rob,' said Mr Willison. 'If you hit it with your left hand and then catch it on the rebound with your right, it's excellent ring training.' He dealt the punch-ball two amateurish blows. 'That's what they call a right cross,' he said.

'I think it's fine. I'll have some fun with it,' said Rob. He watched mildly as his father peeled off the padded mittens.

'Here, slip these on,' said Mr Willison. 'They're just training gloves. They harden your fists. Of course, we can get a pair of proper gloves later. But these are specially for use with the ball.'

'Lunch,' called Mrs Willison from the house.

'Take a punch at it,' Mr Willison urged.

'Let's go and eat.'

'Go on. One punch before you go in. I haven't seen you hit it yet.'

Rob took the gloves, put on the right-hand one, and gave the punch-ball one conscientious blow, aiming at the exact centre.

'Now let's go in,' he said.

'Lunch!'

'All right. We're coming . . .'

'Five feet eight, Rob,' said Mr Willison, folding up the wooden ruler. 'You're taller than I am. This is a great landmark.'

'Only *just* taller.'

'But you're growing all the time. Now all you have to do is to start growing outwards as well as upwards. We'll have you in the middle of that scrum. The heaviest forward in the pack.'

Rob picked up his shirt and began uncertainly poking his arms into the sleeves.

'When do they pick the team?' Mr Willison asked. 'I should have thought they'd have done it by now.'

'They have done it,' said Rob. He bent down to pick up his socks from under a chair.

'They have? And you –'

'I wasn't selected,' said the boy, looking intently at the socks as if trying to detect minute differences in colour and weave.

Mr Willison opened his mouth, closed it again, and stood for a moment looking out of the window. Then he gently laid his hand on his son's shoulder. 'Bad luck,' he said quietly.

'I tried hard,' said Rob quickly.

'I'm sure you did.'

'I played my hardest in the trial games.'

'It's just bad luck,' said Mr Willison. 'It could happen to anybody.'

There was silence as they both continued with their dressing. A faint smell of frying rose into the air, and they could hear Mrs Willison laying the table for breakfast.

'That's it, then, for this season,' said Mr Willison, as if to himself.

'I forgot to tell you, though,' said Rob. 'I was selected for the boxing team.'

'You *were*? I didn't know the school had one.'

'It's new. Just formed. They had some trials for it at the end of last term. I found my punching was better than most people's because I'd been getting plenty of practice with the ball.'

Mr Willison put out a hand and felt Rob's biceps. 'Not bad, not bad at all,' he said critically. 'But if you're going to be a boxer and represent the school, you'll need more power up there. I tell you what. We'll train together.'

'That'll be fun,' said Rob. 'I'm training at school too.'

'What weight do they put you in?'

'It isn't weight, it's age. Under fifteen. Then when you get over fifteen you get classified into weights.'

'Well,' said Mr Willison, tying his tie, 'you'll be in a good position for the under-fifteens. You've got six months to play with. And there's no reason why you shouldn't steadily put muscle on all the time. I suppose you'll be entered as a team, for tournaments and things?'

'Yes. There's a big one at the end of next term. I'll be in that.'

Confident, joking, they went down to breakfast. 'Two eggs for Rob, Mum,' said Mr Willison. 'He's in training. He's going to be a heavyweight.'

'A heavyweight what?' Mrs Willison asked, teapot in hand.

'Boxer,' Rob smiled.

Grace Willison put down the teapot, her lips compressed, and looked from one to the other. '*Boxing?*' she repeated.

'Boxing,' Mr Willison replied calmly.

'Over my dead body,' said Mrs Willison. 'That's one sport I'm definite that he's never going in for.'

'Too late. They've picked him for the under-fifteens. He's had trials and everything.

'Is this true, Rob?' she demanded.

'Yes,' said the boy, eating rapidly.

'Well, you can just tell them you're dropping it. Baroness Summerskill –'

'To hell with Baroness Summerskill!' her husband shouted. 'The first time he gets a chance to do something, the first time he gets picked for a team and given a chance to show what he's made of, and you have to bring up Baroness Summerskill.'

'But it injures their brains! All those blows on the front of the skull. I've read about it –'

'Injures their brains!' Mr Willison snorted. 'Has it injured Ingemar Johansson's brain? Why, he's one of the acutest business men in the world!'

'Rob,' said Mrs Willison steadily, 'when you get to school, go and see the sports master and tell him you're giving up boxing.'

'There isn't a sports master. All the masters do bits of it at different times.'

'There must be one who's in charge of the boxing. All you have to do is tell him –'

'Are you ready, Rob?' said Mr Willison. 'You'll be late for school if you don't go.'

'I'm in plenty of time, Dad. I haven't finished my breakfast.'

'Never mind, push along, old son. You've had your egg and bacon, that's what matters. I want to talk to your mother.'

Cramming a piece of dry toast into his mouth, the boy picked up his satchel and wandered from the room. Husband and wife sat back, glaring hot-eyed at each other.

The quarrel began, and continued for many days. In the end it was decided that Rob should continue boxing until he had repre-sented the school at the tournament in March of the following year, and should then give it up.

'Ninety-six, ninety-seven, ninety-eight, ninety-nine, a hundred,' Mr Willison counted. 'Right, that's it. Now go and take your shower and get into bed.'

'I don't feel tired, honestly,' Rob protested.

'Who's manager here, you or me?' Mr Willison asked bluffly. 'I'm in charge of training and you can't say my methods don't work. Fifteen solid weeks and you start questioning my decisions on the very night of the fight?'

'It just seems silly to go to bed when I'm not –'

'My dear Rob, please trust me. No boxer ever went into a big fight without spending an hour or two in bed, resting, just before going to his dressing-room.'

'All right. But I bet none of the others are bothering to do all this.'

'That's exactly why you're going to be better than the others. Now go and get your shower before you catch cold. Leave the skipping-rope, I'll put it away.'

After Rob had gone, Mr Willison folded the skipping-rope into a neat ball and packed it away in the case that contained the boy's gloves, silk dressing gown, lace-up boxing boots, and trunks with the school badge sewn into the correct position on the right leg. There would be no harm in a little skipping, to limber up and conquer his nervousness while waiting to go on. Humming, he snapped down the catches of the small leather case and went into the house.

Mrs Willison did not lift her eyes from the television set as he entered. 'All ready now, Mother,' said Mr Willison. 'He's going to rest in bed now, and go along at about six o'clock. I'll go with him and wait till the doors open to be sure of a ring-side seat.' He sat down on the sofa beside his wife, and tried to put his arm round her. 'Come on, love,' he said coaxingly. 'Don't spoil my big night.'

She turned to him and he was startled to see her eyes brimming with angry tears. 'What about my big night?' she asked, her voice harsh. 'Fourteen years ago, remember? When he came into the world.'

'Well, what about it?' Mr Willison parried, uneasily aware that the television set was quacking and signalling on the fringe of his attention, turning the scene from clumsy tragedy into a clumsier farce.

'Why didn't you tell me then?' she sobbed. 'Why did you let me have a son if all you were interested in was having him punched to death by a lot of rough bullet-headed louts who —'

'Take a grip on yourself, Grace. A punch on the nose won't hurt him.'

'You're an unnatural father,' she keened. 'I don't know how you can bear to send him into that ring to be beaten and thumped — Oh, why can't you stop him now? Keep him at home? There's no *law* that compels us to —'

'That's where you're wrong, Grace,' said Mr Willison sternly. 'There is a law. The unalterable law of nature that says that the young males of the species indulge in manly trials of strength. Think of all the other lads who are going into the ring tonight. D'you think their mothers are sitting about crying and kicking up a fuss? No — they're proud to have strong, masculine sons who can stand up in the ring and take a few punches.'

147

'Go away, please,' said Mrs Willison, sinking back with closed eyes. 'Just go right away and don't come near me until it's all over.'

'Grace!'

'Please. Please leave me alone. I can't bear to look at you and I can't bear to hear you.'

'You're hysterical,' said Mr Willison bitterly. Rising, he went out into the hall and called up the stairs. 'Are you in bed, Rob?'

There was a slight pause and then Rob's voice called faintly, 'Could you come up, Dad?'

'Come up? Why? Is something the matter?'

'Could you come up?'

Mr Willison ran up the stairs. 'What is it?' he panted. 'D'you want something?'

'I think I've got appendicitis,' said Rob. He lay squinting among the pillows, his face suddenly narrow and crafty.

'I don't believe you,' said Mr Willison shortly. 'I've supervised your training for fifteen weeks and I know you're as fit as a fiddle. You can't possibly have anything wrong with you.'

'I've got a terrible pain in my side,' said Rob. 'Low down on the right-hand side. That's where appendicitis comes, isn't it?'

Mr Willison sat down on the bed. 'Listen, Rob,' he said. 'Don't do this to me. All I'm asking you to do is to go into the ring and have one bout. You've been picked for the school team and everyone's depending on you.'

'I'll die if you don't get the doctor,' Rob suddenly hissed. 'Mum!' he shouted.

Mrs Willison came bounding up the stairs. 'What is it, my pet?'

'My stomach hurts. Low down on the right-hand side.'

'Appendicitis!' She whirled to face Mr Willison. 'That's what comes of your foolishness!'

'I don't believe it,' said Mr Willison. He went out of the bedroom and down the stairs. The television was still jabbering in the living-room, and for fifteen minutes Mr Willison forced himself to sit staring at the strident puppets, glistening in metallic light, as they enacted their Lilliputian rituals. Then he went up to the bedroom again. Mrs Willison was bathing Rob's forehead.

'His temperature's normal,' she said.

'Of course his temperature's normal,' said Mr Willison. 'He doesn't want to fight, that's all.'

'Fetch the doctor,' said a voice from under the cold flannel that swathed Rob's face.

'We will, pet, if you don't get better very soon,' said Mrs Willison, darting a murderous glance at her husband.

Mr Willison slowly went downstairs. For a moment he stood look-ing at the telephone, then picked it up and dialled the number of the grammar school. No one answered. He replaced the receiver, went to the foot of the stairs and called, 'What's the name of the master in charge of this tournament?'

'I don't know,' Rob called weakly.

'You told me you'd been training with Mr Granger,' Mr Willison called. 'Would he know anything about it?'

Rob did not answer, so Mr Willison looked up all the Grangers in the telephone book. There were four in the town, but only one was MA. 'That's him,' said Mr Willison. With lead in his heart and ice in his fingers, he dialled the number.

Mrs Granger fetched Mr Granger. Yes, he taught at the school. He was the right man. What could he do for Mr Willison?

'It's about tonight's boxing tournament.'

'Sorry, what? The line's bad.'

'Tonight's boxing tournament.'

'Have you got the right person?'

'You teach my son, Rob – we've just agreed on that. Well, it's about the boxing tournament he's supposed to be taking part in tonight.'

'Where?'

'Where? At the school, of course. He's representing the under-fifteens.'

There was a pause. 'I'm not quite sure what mistake you're mak-ing, Mr Willison, but I think you've got hold of the wrong end of at least one stick.' A hearty, defensive laugh. 'If Rob belongs to a boxing-club it's certainly news to me, but in any case it can't be anything to do with the school. We don't go in for boxing.'

'Don't go in for it?'

'We don't offer it. It's not in our curriculum.'

'Oh,' said Mr Willison. 'Oh. Thank you. I must have – well, thank you.'

'Not at all. I'm glad to answer any queries. Everything's all right, I trust?'

'Oh, yes,' said Mr Willison, 'yes, thanks. Everything's all right.'

He put down the telephone, hesitated, then turned and began slowly to climb the stairs.

JOHN WAIN

I Didn't Do Nothing

There's only one way to be a good referee. One way. Show 'em you'll stand no nonsense. As soon as a player thinks he can take liberties and get away with it, that's the end. Your authority's gone, and you might as well go home. Referees make me laugh when they say that this player always gives them trouble, or they don't like refereeing in this country, or in that one. As far as I'm concerned, one player's the same as another, and one *country's* the same as another.

I've refereed all over the world: Rome, Berlin, Rio, Paris, and I've never had any real trouble. That time in Montevideo, that was nothing, really; it was just blown up by the press. All those stories about me being hit on the head with a bottle; it just brushed my shoulder, that was all, and as for being smuggled away afterwards in a car, it was the same car I came in.

There may have been one or two stones thrown, but they none of them hit *me*, I can tell you that. Authority, that's all you need, whether it's a British player or a Continental. With foreigners, especially the South Americans, you've got to be a bit firmer, that's all, it's Latin temperament. They come and they throw their arms about and they kiss each other when they score, but in the end it all comes down to the same thing. If they see you're the boss, they'll behave themselves.

There was a match in Santiago. I sent a player off and he wouldn't go. All right, I said, if you won't go, *I'll* go, and I walked off the field and abandoned the match. I'd like you to have seen their faces.

English footballers on the whole don't give you much bother; just the one or two, and we all know who *they* are; you soon learn to look out for them. Mind you, to tell the truth, I've found most of them easy enough. Other referees are always saying to me, 'Look out for so-and-so,' or 'You'd better be careful of so-and-so.'

'Why?' I says, 'he's not a bad lad. He just wants a bit of handling.'

One of them was this young player, Jackie Benbow, of Rovers; he'd been sent off four times before he was twenty, and every referee had an eye out for him. Some people said it was a case of giving a dog a bad name, because of the way he wore his hair; it was blond and long at the back and kind of pointed in that duck's back-side, or whatever you call the style, though as far as I'm concerned, that sort of thing doesn't make any difference.

He was a funny youngster, really, because off the field you wouldn't think he'd say boo to a goose; he was so shy he'd hardly ever open his mouth. Another thing was he was really a very good player, a centre forward, he didn't *need* to be rough, because he had all the ball control.

Well, the first time *I* ever refereed him, he did something in the first ten minutes, and I called him over to me and said, the next time you do that, son, I'm taking your name.

I remember I was surprised because he didn't say anything; just looked at me with a sort of expression as if he couldn't understand it. Half-way through the second half, he was going through for a goal and one of the full-backs came across and slide-tackled him. It was a perfectly good tackle, he took the ball, but when Benbow got up, he deliberately tripped him, he took his feet away. 'Right,' I said, and I got out my notebook. Some referees get it out to threaten a player, but not me, I believe that weakens your authority. If you get it out, you've got to mean it.

'All right,' I said, 'what's your name, son?' and he didn't answer me, he was just sort of staring at me, like he had before. 'You heard me,' I said, 'what's your name?'

Of course, I knew his name all right, but you've got to go through with the formality, and if you ask him his name, he's got to tell you, otherwise you're letting him get away with it. I don't believe in all this turning a player round and looking at the number on his back.

He still didn't speak, so I said, 'Come on, you're holding up the game;' then he looked away from me and he said, 'You know my name.'

'Never mind whether I know it or not,' I said, 'if I ask you, you've got to give it me.' Then he went all red all over his face as if something had embarrassed him, and he mumbled it. I could just make out the 'Benbow', and I wrote it down and I said, 'All right, the next time, you're off.'

I didn't see him again that season, the next time was about September, a midweek game against the Wolves at Molineux. Early on, after a tackle, I saw him turn round and say something to the centre-half, so I ran along beside him – I always believe in that, so long as it's nothing serious – and I said, 'You know me, son, and I know you. Just keep your mouth shut till after the game.' The rest of the match, he was as good as gold.

Well, that's it, I thought. He's learning. He's no different to the rest of them, no worse and no better. If he sees you mean what you say, he'll behave himself.

I had him again three weeks later, this time up in the North in a home match, and there wasn't a thing. After that, I used to read now and again about his being in this incident and that incident, but I didn't blame him, basically, I blamed the referees. It's always the same in football; you keep turning your back on the little things, and sooner or later you get a big thing; somebody blows his top and there's trouble, not only for the player, but for the referee as well. The League don't like it if you get involved in too many disciplinary committees, and the FA notice it, too. I mean it tells its own story, doesn't it?

It wasn't till Christmas I refereed him again. Christmas morning, at Everton. I saw him in the passage there, when I came in. 'Hallo, Benbow,' I said, going past, 'happy Christmas,' but he's slow, the boy, very slow, he just sort of looked at me with his mouth open, and I was in my dressing-room before he'd had time to answer.

It was a hard game, and quite a good one; both sides were in the running for the title, so both of them needed the points. I remember Benbow headed a goal, a very nice one, and it was the first time I'd ever seen him smile, then Everton equalized, and with ten minutes to the end, it was still one-all.

Then Benbow got a ball just beyond the centre circle, he took it past a couple of men, lovely footwork, and it looked as if he'd go right through when the third one brought him down. Benbow got up, and he took a kick at him.

'All right,' I said, 'off!' and I pointed him off towards the dressing-room. Well, I had them all round me in a minute, swarming all round me, Benbow, the captain, two or three of the others. Benbow kept saying, 'It was him! He tripped me!' and he had that same expression on, I recognized it, like the time I took his name, as if he couldn't understand what he'd done wrong. 'Off!' I said. 'Go on!' because if there's one thing I won't have on the field, it's kicking, provocation or no provocation. Let it go, and there's no knowing what you'll have on your hands.

Well, when I got on to the train afterwards, the first person I see, sitting all on his own in a corner of the carriage, is Benbow. He saw me as well, I could tell that by the way he tried to turn his face away, but as far as I'm concerned, that sort of thing's silly; when a match is over, it's over, and besides, I wanted to give him a bit of advice. So I went into the compartment and I sat down beside him and I said, 'Hallo, where are *you* going?'

He didn't look at me, he just mumbled, something which sounded like, 'Home.' I knew he was a Yorkshire boy, so I reckoned they'd let him off, because they were playing at Sheffield next day.

'Well,' I said, 'that was a silly thing you did,' and he said something again, but so quiet you couldn't hear him, and I leaned over close and I said, 'What?' and this time I could just about make it out, he said 'I didn't *do* nothing.'

'Of course you did,' I said. 'You kicked him. You don't think I'd sent you off for nothing. Now look here, son, you're being a fool to yourself. You want to play for England, don't you? Well, *don't* you?' and he said he did. 'Well, what do you think the selectors think when they read about you being sent off, or having your name taken? You don't think they're going to take a chance with you, especially abroad, do you? If you kick somebody abroad, you'll bring the house down. Eh?'

But as I've said, he was a funny lad, it was hard to get an answer from him, he'd go into himself like a shell.

'Listen,' I said, 'have a bit of sense, you'll be suspended for this, you'll probably get a fortnight. You'll lose money, your club have got to play without you, and you're that much farther from getting an England cap. You may have been provoked, I'm not saying you weren't, but as soon as you do anything like that, you put yourself in the wrong, and if you go on doing it, you'll spoil your whole career; I'll tell you, I've seen it happen before. All right, that's enough of that, I'm going out to have my tea. Are you coming?'

He just shook his head, and by the time I got back, he'd disappeared. Still, he seemed to remember what I said, because I must

have refereed him four or five times over the next year, and there was never any trouble at all. He got fourteen days' suspension for the Everton match, like I told him he would, but in those games, I don't remember even giving a foul against him. So when I read now and again about his having his name taken, or when other referees used to complain to me about him, I just used to laugh to myself, because as far as I was concerned, I could tell it was six of one and half a dozen of the other.

Early this season, I took Rover's game against Sheffield Wednesday.

It was a tough game, both sides going hard, and just about on the half-hour, there was a dust-up, nothing very serious, between Benbow and one of the Wednesday defence. I went over there and I said, 'Look, son, you remember me, we want none of that today.' And the next thing he did was he hit me, he hit me right below the eye; he was walking off the field before I'd even got up off the ground.

Indefinite

Sine die suspension he got for that. He'll be lucky if he ever plays again, *I* can tell you.

BRIAN GLANVILLE

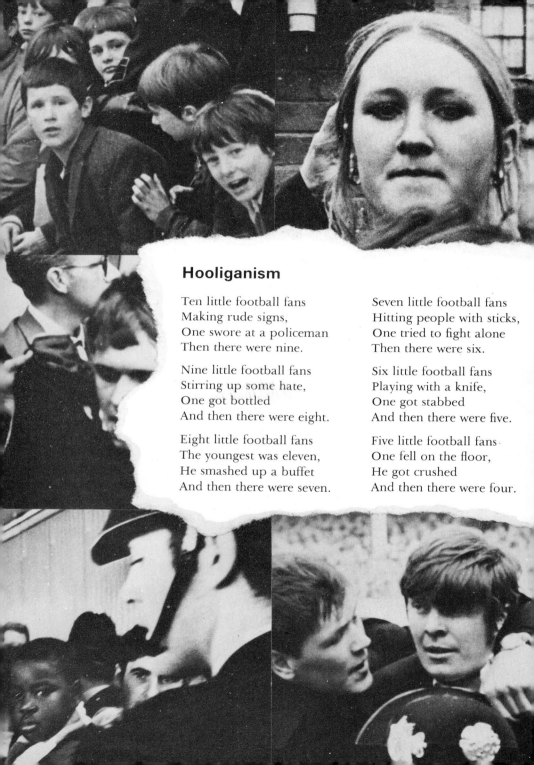

Hooliganism

Ten little football fans
Making rude signs,
One swore at a policeman
Then there were nine.

Nine little football fans
Stirring up some hate,
One got bottled
And then there were eight.

Eight little football fans
The youngest was eleven,
He smashed up a buffet
And then there were seven.

Seven little football fans
Hitting people with sticks,
One tried to fight alone
Then there were six.

Six little football fans
Playing with a knife,
One got stabbed
And then there were five.

Five little football fans
One fell on the floor,
He got crushed
And then there were four.

Four little football fans
Just like you and me,
One threw a penny at the goalie
Then there were three.

Three little football fans
The other team did boo,
But the fans outnumbered them
Then there were two.

Two little football fans
After all was done
One ran on the football pitch
Then there was one.

One little football fan
Glad his team had won,
Argued with some other fans
Then there were none.

PETER KETT

How to Kill Your Form Master

JOHN   Stop! *[Silence]* Very well. You have had your warning. The form will stay in this afternoon from half past two until I am satisfied with your behaviour.
[Pause]

CLOISTERMOUTH   It's not a good idea, sir.

JOHN   No. Cloistermouth? Tell me why not.

CLOISTERMOUTH   Well, sir, Mr Pelham did it once.

CUTHBUN   The week before last, sir.

CLOISTERMOUTH   And that was why we killed him.
[Dead silence]

JOHN   Cloistermouth, take this note to the headmaster.

CLOISTERMOUTH   Now, sir?

JOHN   At once.

CLOISTERMOUTH   What does it say, sir?

JOHN	That you have been insolent.
CLOISTERMOUTH	But, sir, I haven't. Only truthful.
OMNES	That's right, sir.
JOHN	Go on, Cloistermouth.
CLOISTERMOUTH	No, sir.
JOHN	Very well. Then I shall fetch the headmaster here.
CLOISTERMOUTH	You'll look an awful fool, sir.
JOHN	*[Shouting]* Get out!
CLOISTERMOUTH	If you hit me, sir, there'll be a terrific row.
TERHEW	Form masters aren't allowed to hit us.
CUTHBUN	You'll be sacked.
AGGERIDGE	And after all, he was telling the truth, sir.
CLOISTERMOUTH	I always do.
JOHN	Oh yes? And how did you kill Mr Pelham?
LIPSTROB	We murdered him.
CLOISTERMOUTH	On Signal Cliff, sir.
CUTHBUN	That's the big one on this side of the town.
CLOISTERMOUTH	He always went there for a walk in the afternoon, sir. The day after he'd kept us in we waited for him.
TERHEW	Six of us.
CUTHBUN	In the bushes.
CLOISTERMOUTH	He came up quite slowly, panting a bit.
TERHEW	And he paused at the top and took out his handkerchief.
CUTHBUN	The fog was coming in from the sea.
CLOISTERMOUTH	Then we came out from the bushes all round him. He started to say something. . . .
LIPSTROB	But we rushed him and got him on the ground.
AGGERIDGE	Rugger tackle.
CLOISTERMOUTH	His specs fell off and he started lashing out.
BUNGABINE	So we hit him on the head with a stone.

ORRIS	KO.
LIPSTROB	Gedoing!
TERHEW	Then we carried him to the edge and chucked him over.
BUNGABINE	A'one, a'two, a'three . . . and away!
CLOISTERMOUTH	And there was blood on the stone, so we threw that over too.
ORRIS	Dead easy.
CUTHBUN	Nobody saw us because of the fog.
BUNGABINE	The perfect crime. Haw haw haw.
JOHN	Hardly.
CUTHBUN	Why not, sir?
JOHN	If you had done it. . . .
OMNES	We did.
JOHN	You would have spoilt it all by telling me. Your vanity would have given you away.
CLOISTERMOUTH	But we have told you, sir.
JOHN	And if I believed you I'd tell the police . . . through the headmaster of course.
CUTHBUN	But that wouldn't do any good, sir. You don't know which of us did it.
JOHN	The police would find out. They'd get you one by one and question you.
TERHEW	We've all got alibis, sir.
CLOISTERMOUTH	Yes, sir, really we have. I was in Chapel with Unman and Muffet, polishing the candlesticks.
CUTHBUN	Terhew, Hogg and me were having tea in Orris's study.
LIPSTROB	Aggeridge, Root and Trindle were playing fives with me.
BUNGABINE	I was in the armoury with Borby and Ankerton. We were cleaning our equipment web for the CCF parade.
WITTERING	And Mudd and Munn and me were doing detention.
CUTHBUN	I mean to say, sir, we can prove it. There are at least two witnesses for every member of the form.

GILES COOPER *Unman, Wittering and Zigo*

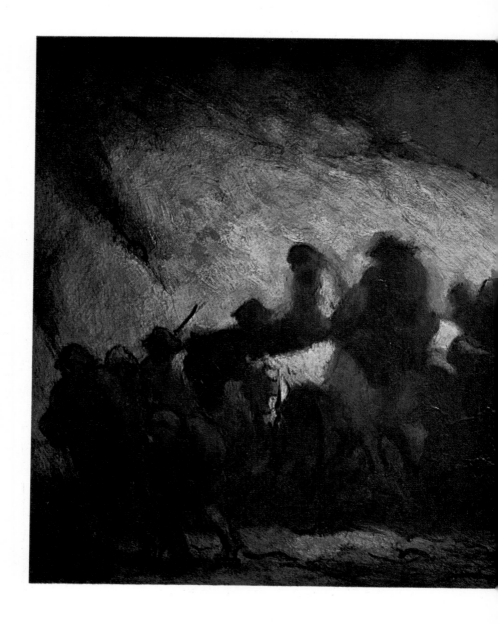

Children's Crusade 1939

In 'thirty-nine, in Poland
a bloody battle took place,
turning many a town and village
into a wilderness.

The sister lost her brother,
the wife her husband in war,
the child between fire and rubble
could find his parents no more.

From Poland no news was forthcoming
neither letter nor printed word,
but in all the Eastern countries
a curious tale can be heard.

Snow fell when they told one another
this tale in an Eastern town
of a children's crusade that started
in Poland, in 'thirty-nine.

Along the highroads in squadrons
these hungry children tripped,
and on their way picked up others
in villages gutted and stripped.

They wanted to flee from the fighting
so that the nightmare would cease
and one day at last they'd arrive in
a country where there was peace.

They had a little leader
who was their prop and stay.
This leader had one great worry:
he did not know the way.

A girl of eleven carried
a toddler of four without cease,
lacking nothing that makes a mother
but a country where there was peace.

A little Jewish boy marched in the troop,
with velvet collar and cuff,
he was used to the whitest of bread
and he fought bravely enough.

And two brothers joined this army,
each a mighty strategist,
these took an empty cottage by storm
with nothing but rain to resist.

And a lean grey fellow walked there,
by the roadside, in isolation,
and bore the burden of terrible guilt:
he came from a Nazi legation.

There was a musician among them
who in a shelled village found a drum one day
and was not allowed to strike it,
so as not to give them away.

And there was also a dog,
caught for the knife at the start,
yet later kept on as an eater
because no one had the heart.

And they had a school there also,
and a small teacher who knew how to yell,
and a pupil against the wall of a shot-up tank
as far as peac . . . learned to spell.

And there was a concert too:
by a roaring winter stream one lad
was allowed to beat the drum,
But no one heard him. Too bad.

And there was a love affair.
She was twelve, he was fifteen.
In a secluded courtyard
she combed his hair.

This love could not last long,
too cold the weather came on.
How can the little tree flower
with so much snow coming down?

And there was a war as well,
for there was another crowd beside this
and the war only came to an end
because it was meaningless.

But when the war still raged
around a shelled pointsman's hut,
suddenly, so they say, one party
found their food supply had been cut.

And when the other heard this, they sent
a man to relieve their plight
with a sack of potatoes, because
without food one cannot fight.

There was a trial too,
with a pair of candles for light,
and after much painful examining
the judge was found guilty that night.

And a funeral too: of a boy
with velvet on collar and wrist;
it was two Poles and two Germans
carried him to his rest.

Protestant, Catholic and Nazi were there
when his body to earth they were giving,
and at the end a little Socialist spoke
of the future of the living.

So there was faith and hope,
only no meat and no bread,
and let no man blame them if they stole a few things
when he offered no board or bed.

And let no man blame the needy man
who offered no bread or rice,
for with fifty to feed it's a matter
of flour, not self-sacrifice.

They made for the south in the main.
The south is where the sun
at midday, twelve o'clock sharp
lies straight in front of one.

True, they found a soldier
who wounded on fir-needles lay.
They nursed him for seven days
so he could show them the way.

He told them: To Bilgoray!
Delirious, surely, far gone,
and he died on the eighth day.
They buried him too, and moved on.

And there were sign-posts also,
though snow rubbed the writing out;
only they'd ceased to point the way,
having been turned about.

This was not for a practical joke,
but on a military ground,
and when they looked for Bilgoray
the place was not to be found.

They stood around their leader
who looked up at the snowy air
and, extending his little hand,
said, it must be over there.

Once, at night, they saw a fire,
but better not go, they decided.
Once three tanks rolled past them,
each with people inside it.

Once, too, they came to a city,
and skirted it, well out of sight;
till they'd left it well behind them
they only marched on at night.

In what used to be South-East Poland
when snow swept the landscape clean
that army of fifty-five children
was last seen.

If I close my eyes and try,
I can see them trudge on
from one shell-blasted homestead
to another shell-blasted one.

Above them, in the cloudy spaces,
I see new long trains progress,
painfully trudging in the cold wind's face,
homeless, directionless.

Looking for the country at peace
without fire and thunder's blast,
not like that from which they have come;
and the train grows vast.

And soon in the flickering half-light
no longer the same it seemed:
other little faces I saw,
Spanish, French, yellow ones gleamed.

That January, in Poland
a stray dog was caught;
hanging from its lean neck
a cardboard notice it brought.

It read: please come and help us!
We no longer know the way.
There are fifty-five of us.
The dog won't lead you astray.

Don't shoot him dead.
Only he knows the place.
With him
our very last hope you'd efface.

The writing was in a child's hand.
By farmers it was read.
Since then a year and a half have passed.
The dog, who was starving, is dead.

BERTOLT BRECHT *translated from the German by*
Michael Hamburger

2000 Years Old

An early spring day – 8 May 1950. Evening was gathering over Tollund Fen in Bjaeldskov Dal. Momentarily, the sun burst in, bright and yet subdued, through a gate in blue thunder-clouds in the west, bringing everything mysteriously to life. The evening stillness was only broken, now and again, by the grating love-call of the snipe. The dead man, too, deep down in the umber-brown peat, seemed to have come alive. He lay on his damp bed as though asleep, resting on his side, the head inclined a little forward, arms and legs bent. His face wore a gentle expression – the eyes lightly closed, the lips softly pursed, as if in silent prayer. It was as though the dead man's soul had for a moment returned from another world, through the gate in the western sky.

The dead man who lay there was 2000 years old. A few hours earlier he had been brought out from the sheltering peat by two men who, their spring sowing completed, had now to think of the cold winter days to come, and were occupied in cutting peat for the tile stove and kitchen range.

As they worked, they suddenly saw in the peat-layer a face so fresh that they could only suppose they had stumbled on a recent murder.

P. V. GLOB *The Bog People*

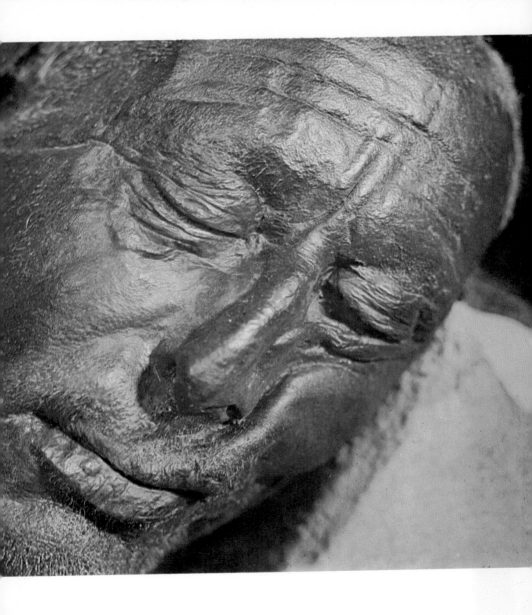

AN APPLICATION

I ask respectfully to be given the government
of the world.
The reasons for my application are that I am
a better, wiser, and more individual man than
anyone else.
I declare that our district is poor and our
ᵐxxxᵐ market days have been abolished because
there will be industrialisation. In my house, too,
things are not too ᵖᵢxᵐᵢ plentiful, because my
son-in-law has eight other people to ᵐᵐ support,
apart from myself, two of them intellectuals.
My application, therefore, cannot be supported
by money or by armed might. That is why I ask to
be released from the duty to have atomic weapons.
If need be I can produce the necessary certificate
from my parish.
I understand that in these circumstances it will
not be easy to give me ᵐᵐ supreme power. But I am
ₓₓₜₖₙₓₓₙₖₖₙₓₓₜₓₓₙₓₓₙₙₓₜₙ not losing hope that my
request will find support in the enthusiasm of
nations and the development of history. I am also
counting on Providence.
First, as I have said already, I am better than all
other men. It is quite likely that some will dispute
this claim that it is they who are better. Their
arguments, however, are without validity because they
are not me and so they cannot know how good I am.
In my opinion it would be better for everybody if I
became the ruler of the world. I am ready to make
sacrifices and that is the reason I can undertake
this xxxx task. When I was young it might have been
different, but now I have come into my own and I can
lead.
Here at home we have not got a single battleship. We
cannot even afford a colander and my poor daughter
strains the dumplings the best she can. So what? You
rule the world because you are the best and not the
strongest. Everybody who has an army claims it is a
pure coincidence. Nobody wants to rule the world
because he has an army but because he is the best man.

So my chances must be at least equal, If not greater,
because I have no army and I am the best. What use is
a warship to me? It would be an unnecessary expense and
also in the way at home, especially now that my
daughter is expecting again.
I am not concerned about myself, but about humanity.
Often, when I hide in my little garden, and, thank
God, I still have a garden, when I pick a red currant
and then a whole bunch of them, something prods me,
like with a finger. "You pick the red currants, but
what about humanity?" It is then that I feel like
abandoning everything and becoming the ruler.
  Yesterday my son-in-law locked me up because, he
said, I eat too much. That is why I have a little
free time to write this application. I have been
meaning to do it for a long time, but flies have
been drowning in the ink bottle and it was unpleasant
to dip the pen. Now that autumn has come there xxxxxxxxx
seem to be fxxx fewer flies.
  Just as well that I am myself and nobody else is me.
It is a frightening thought that I might have been
someone else, and I would then be looking at myself
and not know what sort of man I was.
  My son-in-law is coming. I xxxxxx understand that
xxxx everything costs money, but ixxxxx is it
necessary to start beating immediately?
  I am awaiting a favourable answer to my application.

SLAWOMIR MROZEK *translated from the Polish by Konrad Sy*

Missionary

A harsh entry I had of it, Grasud;
the tiny shuttle strained to its limits
by radiation belts, dust-storms,
not to mention the pitiless heat which
hit it on plunging into the atmosphere
– its fire-shield clean vaporized; and then,
on landing, the utter cold and stillness
of a mountain-slope, cedar-trees and
what they call

snow. As I went numbly through the
routine I could do in my sleep –
mentalizing myself, smothering
my body and the shuttle in a
defensive neutrino-screen, hiding them
securely in the snow,
I looked up and, between the branches
of the cedars, could see
the mother-ship sliding away through
the dark, like an unfixed star, westwards
to its other destinations: that was
the worst moment of all, Grasud! I'd have

called it back! So lonely, such an alien
world they'd left me in. Goodbye, Lagash!
goodbye, Theremon! fare well! (But no
voice now even to make a gesture against
the silence.)
   Then the agonizingly slow
descent, towards the village,
my spirit dark, already missing
not only Theremon and Lagash, but
that other friend, my body's familiar
chemistry. By now I felt my
vaunted courage ebbing, Grasud; I think
those years of training
alone forced me to go on, into the village,
into the houses, inns, into
– after much vain searching – a ripened
womb; there superseding
(not without a pang) its foetus-spirit.
How black that airlock,
after the six suns of our own system,
I needn't tell you. Even space,
in recollection, seemed a blaze of
supernovas. But I settled to my task,
wrestling to get on terms with carbon
compounds fearsomely different from
the synthetic ones I'd practised in.
Of course, as I was born and the years
passed, it seemed as natural to go
on man's two legs as on our Vardian
limbs. But when these pains eased,
one far bitterer grew: my seeds were cast
on stony ground; the more
I exhorted,
– the more I spoke, obliquely, of
the many mansions of our Vardian
Commonwealth, and of the place
that could be theirs – the more it
seemed those simple, instinctive creatures
lied, stole, slandered, fornicated,
killed. . . . Grasud, how often, sick with
failure, only the words of Vrak
sustained me – 'a world lies in your hands.'
That was the time he

exploding stars

sent for the three of us when
all ears were ringing with the news of
the three life-planets found in
NTD 1065. If we had hopes,
we masked them. His words to us, for
all that's happened, I'll hoard always.
'Thoorin, Lagash, Theremon,' I hear him
saying, 'I'm sending *you* . . . you're young,
but this is what you've trained for, bio-
enlightenment. You've done well.'
And then – 'a world lies in your hands'.
So, Grasud, I toiled. In the end
I tried too hard; the time of space-
rendezvous was almost come. Anyway,
they killed me. I loved them, and they
killed me.
    Yes, it was hard,
as you can well imagine,
on the return-journey, to avoid feeling
the faintest warp of
jealousy, as Theremon and
Lagash talked with
the happy emissaries of their
planets. – What does Vrak say? He is
kind, promises – after this loathsome
rest – another
chance, though not of course on that
planet. My 'inability' (he avoids
the word failure) to raise them
ethically to the point where we could
safely announce ourselves, proves, he
says, there's no point trying again
for a few thousand years. Meanwhile,
he suggests, maybe some of my words
will start to bear fruit. . . . He is kind!
His last words were 'Forget about it,
Thoorin; enjoy your stay on
Atar.' Forget!
with the relaxed faces of my friends a
perpetual thorn.

D. M. THOMAS

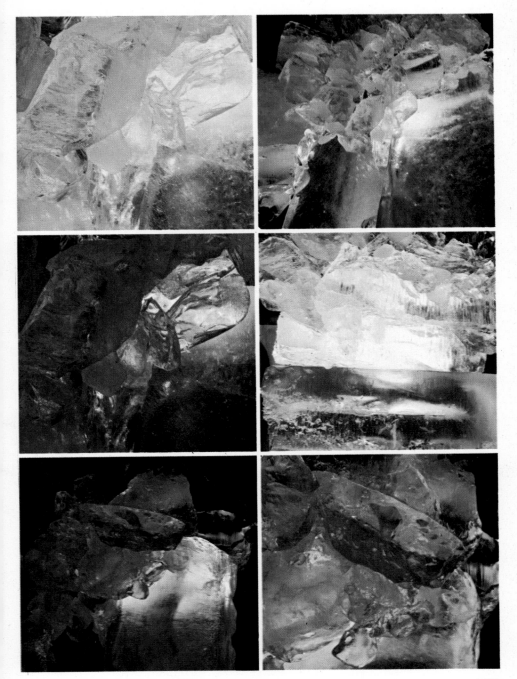

The End of the World

Some say the world will end in fire,
Some say in ice,
ROBERT FROST

The thick furs thudded softly to the ground as Professor Millward jerked himself upright on the narrow bed. This time, he was sure, it had been no dream: the freezing air that rasped against his lungs still seemed to echo with the sound that had come crashing out of the night.

He gathered his furs around him and listened intently. All was quiet again: from the narrow windows on the western walls long shafts of moonlight played upon the endless rows of books, as they played upon the dead city beneath. The world was utterly still: even in the old days the city would have been silent on such a night, and it was doubly silent now.

Still dazed with sleep, Professor Millward shuffled out of bed, and doled a few lumps of coke into the glowing brazier. Then he made his way slowly towards the nearest window, pausing now and then to rest his hand lovingly on the volumes he had guarded all these years.

He shielded his eyes from the brilliant moonlight and peered out into the night. The sky was cloudless: the sound he had heard had not been thunder, whatever it might have been. It had come from the north, and, even as he waited, it came again.

Distance had softened it, distance and the bulk of the hills that lay beyond London. It did not race across the sky like thunder, but seemed to come from a single point far to the north. It was like no natural sound that Professor Millward had ever heard, and for a moment he dared to hope again.

Only Man, he was sure, could have made such a sound. Perhaps the dream that had kept him here among these treasures of civilization for more than twenty years would soon be a dream no longer. Men were returning to England, blasting their way through the ice and snow with the weapons which science had given them before the coming of the Dust. It was strange that they should come by land, and from the north, but he thrust aside any thoughts that might quench the newly kindled flame of hope.

Three hundred feet below, the broken sea of snow-covered roofs lay bathed in the bitter moonlight. Miles away the tall stacks of Battersea Power Station glimmered like thin white ghosts beneath the night sky. Now that the dome of St Paul's had collapsed beneath the weight of snow, they alone challenged his supremacy.

Professor Millward walked slowly back along the bookshelves, thinking over the plan that had formed in his mind. Twenty years ago he had watched the last helicopters climbing heavily out of Regent's Park, their rotors churning the ceaselessly falling snow. Even then, when the silence had closed around him, he could not bring himself to believe that the north had been abandoned forever. Yet already he had waited a whole generation, among the books to which he dedicated his life.

In those early days he had sometimes heard, over the radio which was his only contact with the south, of the struggle to colonize the now temperate lands of the equator. He did not know the outcome of that far-off battle, fought with desperate skill in the dying jungles and across deserts that had already felt the first touch of snow. Perhaps it had failed: the radio had been silent now for fifteen years or more. Yet if men and machines were indeed returning from the north – of all directions – he might again be able to hear their voices as they spoke to one another and to the lands from which they had come.

Professor Millward left the university building perhaps a dozen times a year, and then only through sheer necessity. Over the past two decades he had collected everything he needed from the shops in the Bloomsbury area, for in the final exodus vast supplies of stock had been left behind through lack of transport. In many ways, indeed, his life could be called luxurious: certainly no professor of English literature had ever been clothed with such expensive garments as those he had taken from an Oxford Street furrier's.

The sun was blazing from a cloudless sky as he shouldered his pack and unlocked the massive gates. Up to ten years ago packs of starving dogs had hunted in this area, and though he had seen none for years he was still cautious and always carried a revolver when he went into the open.

The sunlight was so brilliant that the reflected glare hurt his eyes: but it was almost wholly lacking in heat. Although the belt of cosmic dust through which the planets were now passing had made little visible difference to the sun's brightness, it had robbed it of all strength. No one knew whether the world would swim out into the warmth again in ten or a thousand years, and civilization had fled southward in search of lands where the word 'summer' was not an empty mockery.

The latest drifts had packed hard and Professor Millward had little difficulty in making the journey to Tottenham Court Road. Sometimes it had taken him hours of floundering through the snow and one year he had been sealed in his great concrete watchtower for nine months on end.

He kept away from the houses with their dangerous burdens of snow and their hanging icicles, and went north a hundred yards until he found the shop he was seeking. The words above the shattered windows were still bright and clear: 'Thos. Jenkins & Sons. Radio and Electrical. Television a Specialty.'

Some snow had drifted through a broken section of roofing, but the little upstairs room had not altered since his last visit a dozen years ago. The short-wave radio still stood on the table, and the empty tins scattered on the floor spoke mutely of the lonely hours he had spent here before all hope had died. He wondered if he must go through the same ordeal again.

Professor Millward brushed the snow from the copy of *The Amateur Radio Handbook for 1955*, which had taught him what little he knew about wireless. The test meters and batteries were still lying in their half-remembered places, and to his relief some of the batteries still held their charge. He searched through the stock until he had built up the necessary power supplies, and checked the radio as well as he could. Then he was ready.

It was a pity he could never send the manufacturers the testimonial they deserved. The faint 'hiss' from the speaker brought back memories of the BBC, of the nine o'clock news and symphony concerts, of all the things he had once taken for granted in a world that was now gone like a dream. With scarcely controlled impatience he tuned across the wave bands, but everywhere there was nothing except that scarcely audible hiss. It was disappointing, but no more: he remembered that the real test would come at night. In the meantime he would forage among the surrounding shops for anything that might be useful.

It was dusk when he returned to the little room. A hundred miles above his head, tenuous and invisible, the Heaviside Layer would be expanding outwards towards the stars as the sun went down. So it had done every evening for millions of years, and for a half-century only Man had used it for his own purposes, to reflect around the world his messages of hate or peace, to echo with trivialities or to sound with the music that had once been called immortal.

Slowly, with infinite patience, Professor Millward began to search the wave bands that a generation ago had been a babel of shouting voices and stabbing Morse. Even as he listened, the faint hope he had dared to cherish began to fade within him. The city itself was no more silent than the once-crowded oceans of ether. Only the faint crackle of thunderstorms half the world away broke the intolerable stillness. Man had abandoned his latest conquest.

Soon after midnight the batteries faded out. Professor Millward did not have the heart to search for more, but curled up in his furs and fell into a troubled sleep. He got what consolation he could from the knowledge that, if he had not proved his theory, neither had he disproved it.

The heatless sunlight was flooding the lonely white road when he began the homeward journey. He was very tired, for he had slept little and his sleep had been broken by the recurring fantasy of rescue.

The silence was suddenly broken by the distant thunder that came rolling over the white roofs. It came – there could be no doubt now – from beyond the northern hills that had once been London's playground. From the buildings on either side, little avalanches of snow went swishing out into the wide street: then the silence returned.

Professor Millward stood motionless – weighing, considering, analysing. The sound had been too-long-drawn to be an ordinary explosion. Perhaps – or was he dreaming again? – it was nothing less than the distant thunder of an atomic bomb, burning and blasting away the snow a million tons at a time, and bringing life instead of death. His hopes revived, and the disappointments of the night began to fade.

That momentary pause almost cost him his life. Out of a side street, something huge and white moved suddenly into his field of vision. For a moment his mind refused to accept the reality of what he saw: then the paralysis left him and he fumbled desperately for his futile revolver. Padding towards him across the snow, swinging its head from side to side with a hypnotic, serpentine motion, was a polar bear.

He dropped his belongings and ran, floundering over the snow towards the nearest buildings. Providentially, the Underground entrance was only fifty feet away. The steel grille was closed, but he remembered breaking the lock many years ago. The temptation to look back was almost intolerable, for he could hear nothing to tell how near his pursuer was.

For one frightful moment the iron lattice resisted his numbed fingers. Then it yielded reluctantly and he forced his way through the narrow opening.

Out of his childhood there came a sudden, incongruous memory of an albino ferret he had once seen weaving its body ceaselessly across the wire netting of its cage. There was the same reptile grace in the monstrous shape, twice as high as a man, that reared itself in baffled fury against the grille. The metal bowed but did not yield beneath the pressure: then the bear dropped to the ground, grunted softly, and padded away. It slashed once or twice at the fallen haver-sack, scattering a few tins of food into the snow, and vanished as silently as it had come.

A very shaken Professor Millward reached the university three hours later, after moving in short spurts from one refuge to the next. After all these years, he was no longer alone in the city. He wondered if there were other visitors, and that same night he knew the answer. Just before dawn he heard, quite distinctly, the cry of a wolf from somewhere in the direction of Hyde Park.

By the end of the week he knew that the animals of the north were on the move. Once he saw a reindeer running southward, pursued by a pack of silent wolves, and sometimes in the night there were sounds of deadly conflict. He was amazed that so much life had managed to exist in the white wilderness between London and the Pole. Now something was driving it southward, and the knowledge brought him a mounting excitement. He did not believe that these fierce survivors would flee from anything save Man.

The strain of waiting was beginning to affect Professor Millward's mind, and for hours he would sit in the cold sunlight, his furs wrapped around him, dreaming of rescue and thinking of the ways in which men might be returning to England. Perhaps an expedition had come from North America across the Atlantic ice: it might have been years upon its way. But why had it come so far north? His favourite theory was that the Atlantic ice packs were not thick enough for heavy traffic farther to the south.

One thing, however, he could not explain to his satisfaction. There had been no air reconnaissance, and it was hard to believe that the art of flight had been lost in so short a time.

Occasionally he would walk along the ranks of books, whispering now and then to a well-loved volume. There were books here that he had not dared to open for years, they reminded him so poignantly of the past. But now, as the days grew longer and brighter, he would sometimes take down a volume of poetry and reread his old favourites. Then he would go to the tall windows and shout the magic words over the roof tops, as if they would break the spell that had gripped the world.

It was warmer now, as if the ghosts of lost summers had returned to haunt the land. For whole days the temperature rose above freezing, while in many places flowers were breaking through the snow. Whatever was approaching from the north was nearer, and puzzling several times a day that enigmatic roar would go thundering over the city, sending the snow sliding upon a thousand roofs. There were strange, grinding undertones that Professor Millward found baffling and even ominous. At times it was almost as if he were listening to the clash of mighty armies, and sometimes a mad and dreadful thought came into his mind and would not be dismissed. Often he would wake in the night and imagine that he heard the sound of mountains moving to the sea.

So the summer wore away, and as the sound of that distant battle drew steadily nearer, Professor Millward was the prey of ever more violently alternating hopes and fears. Although he saw no more wolves or bears – they seemed to have fled southward – he did not risk leaving the safety of his fortress. Every morning he would climb to the highest window of the tower and search the northern horizon with field glasses. But all he ever saw was the stubborn retreat of the snows above Hampstead, as they fought their bitter rear-guard action against the sun.

His vigil ended with the last days of the brief summer. The grinding thunder in the night had been nearer than ever before, but there was still nothing to hint at its real distance from the city. Professor Millward felt no premonition as he climbed to the narrow window and raised his binoculars to the northern sky.

As a watcher from the walls of some threatened fortress might have seen the sunlight glinting on the first spears of an advancing army, so in that moment Professor Millward knew the truth. The air was crystal clear, and the hills were sharp and brilliant against the cold blue of the sky. They had lost almost all their snow: once he would have rejoiced at that, but it meant nothing now.

Overnight, the enemy he had forgotten had conquered the last defences and was preparing for the final onslaught. As he saw that deadly glitter along the crest of the doomed hills, Professor Millward understood at last the sound he had heard advancing for so many months. It was little wonder that he had dreamed of mountains on the march.

Out of the north, their ancient home, returning in triumph to the lands they had once possessed, the glaciers had come again.

ARTHUR C. CLARKE

Little Johnny's Final Letter

Mother,
I won't be home this evening, so
don't worry; don't hurry to report me missing.
Don't drain the canals to find me,
I've decided to stay alive, don't
search the woods, I'm not hiding,
simply gone to get myself classified.
Don't leave my shreddies out,
I've done with security.
Don't circulate my photograph to society
I have disguised myself as a man
and am giving priority to obscurity.
It suits me fine:
I have taken off my short trousers
and put on long ones, and
now am going out into the city, so
don't worry; don't hurry to report me missing.

I've rented a room without any curtains
and sit behind the windows growing cold,
heard your plea on the radio this morning,
you sounded sad and strangely old. . . .

BRIAN PATTEN

Acknowledgements

For permission to use copyright material acknowledgement is made to the following:

Stories   For 'Children's Crusade 1939' by Bertolt Brecht from *Tales From The Calendar* to Methuen Company Ltd and Suhrkamp Verlag; for 'In the Factory' by Philip Callow from *Native Ground* to the author; for 'The End of the World' by Arthur C. Clarke from *Reach For Tomorrow* to the author; for 'How to Kill Your Form Master' by Giles Cooper from *Unman, Wittering and Zigo* to the author and BBC Publications Ltd; for 'Sunset' by William Faulkner from *New Orleans Sketches* to Chatto & Windus and Random House Inc.; for 'I Didn't Do Nothing' by Brian Glanville from *Goalkeepers Are Crazy* to Jonathan Cape Ltd; for '2000 Years Old' by P. V. Glob from *The Bog People* to Faber & Faber Ltd and Cornell University Press; for 'Proudly, My Son' by E. A. Gollschewsky to the author; for 'The Big Decision' by Lesley Anne Hayes to the Daily Mirror Children's Literary Competition; for 'The Huge Footprint' by Bernard Heuvelmans from *On The Track of Unknown Animals* to Granada Publishing Ltd and Hill & Wang Inc.; for 'Sunday' by Ted Hughes from *Wodwo* to Harper & Row Inc. and Faber & Faber Ltd; for 'Flame on the Frontier' by Dorothy M. Johnson to McIntosh & Otis Inc. and Dodd, Mead & Company; for 'Hooliganism' by Peter Kett from *Stepney Words* to the author; for 'A Mild Attack of Locusts' by Doris Lessing from *A Habit of Loving* to Curtis Brown Ltd and Thomas Y. Crowell; for 'An Application' by Slawomir Mrozek translated by Konrad Syrop from *Ugupu Bird* to Macdonald & Company Ltd and Grove Press Inc.; for 'The Man who was Shorter than Himself' by Kenneth Patchen from *Doubleheader* to New Directions Publishing Corporation; for 'Little Johnny's Final Letter' by Brian Patten from *Little Johnny's Confession* to George Allen & Unwin Ltd and Hill & Wang Inc.; for 'The Saturday Dance' from *The Mating Season* by Alan Plater published in *Worth A Hearing* to the author and Blackie & Son Ltd; for 'You Should have Seen the Mess' by Muriel Spark from *The Go-Away Bird and Other Stories* to Harold Ober Associates Inc.; for 'An Interview with the Youth Careers Officer' by Peter Terson from *Zigger Zagger* to Penguin Books Ltd; for 'Missionary' by D. M. Thomas from *Penguin Modern Poets II* to Penguin Books Ltd; for 'Accident' by Leonard Thompson from *Akenfield* to Penguin Books Ltd; for 'The Peacelike Mongoose' by James Thurber from *Fables For Our Time* to Helen Thurber and Harper & Row Inc.; for 'The Pious Lion' from *Folktales of England* to University of Chicago Press; for 'First Frost' by Andrei Voznesensky from *Antiworlds* to Oxford University Press and Basic Books Inc.; for 'Manhood' by John Wain from *Death Of The Hind Legs* to Curtis Brown Ltd and Viking Press Inc.; for 'I Remember . . .' by Lynne Whitehead to the author.

Pictures   For the pictures on pages 6–8 to Mr S. Clamp; pages 10–11 from *And Miss Carter Wore Pink* by Helen Bradley to the artist and Jonathan Cape Ltd; pages 12–13 to Euan Duff; pages 22–3 to the Alberto Giacometti Foundation, Kunsthaus Zurich; pages 24–5 from *The Man Who Drew the Twentieth Century* edited by Michael Bateman with drawings by H. M. Bateman to the artist and London Management; page 26 to Mark Edwards; pages 30–31 to Arthur Boyd; pages 34–5 to Sir Russell Drysdale, Private Collections; page 44 from *Hurrah for Anything* by Kenneth Patchen to the artist and New Directions Publishing Corporation; pages 46–7 to the Brooklyn Museum, New York; pages 50–51 to Paul Oliver; page 57 to *Time Out*; pages 58–9 to Novosti Press; pages 62–3 to Gianni Tortoli; page 64 to FAO; pages 72–3, 82–3 to Ron Chapman; pages 74–5 to Chris Steele-Perkins; page 88 to the Leo Castelli Gallery and Milwaukee Art Gallery; pages 92–3 to Karlheinz Klübescheidt; page 94 to Kingston Local History Museum; pages 112–13, 117 to Cinema Center Films; page 118 to Aberdeen University; page 125 to the Photographer and Rapho; page 126 to Mr Eglon Shaw, The Sutcliffe Gallery; pages 138–9 to the Mansell Collection; page 140 from *Fables of our Time*, published by Harper & Row Inc. to Mrs Thurber; page 150 to The Solomon R. Guggenheim Museum; page 158 to Paramount Pictures Ltd; pages 162–3 to the Musée de Petit Palais; page 169 to P. Boucas WHO; page 171 to Barry Hicks and Healey Agency; pages 174–5 to Snark International, Collection Roland Penrose; pages 178–9 to Geoffrey Drury; page 187 to Richard Hamilton, Collection Edwin Janss Jr.

List of Illustrations

Index of Authors and Translators